Wyoming Bucket List Adventure Guide

Explore 100 Offbeat Destinations You Must Visit!

Leslie Crawford

Canyon Press
canyon@purplelink.org

Please consider writing a review!
Just visit: purplelink.org/review

ISBN: 978-1-957590-19-6

FREE BONUS

Discover 31 Incredible Places You Can
Visit Next! Just Go To:

purplelink.org/travel

Table of Contents:

Cheyenne

Cody

How to Use This Book

Welcome to your very own adventure guide to exploring the many wonders of the state of Wyoming. Not only does this book offer the most wonderful places to visit and sights to see in the vast state, but it provides GPS coordinates for Google Maps to make exploring that much easier.

Adventure Guide
Sorted by region, this guide offers over 100 amazing wonders found in Wyoming for you to see and explore. They can be visited in any order and this book will help you keep track of where you've been and where to look forward to going next. Each section describes the area or place, what to look for, how to get there, and what you may need to bring along.

GPS Coordinates
As you can imagine, not all of the locations in this book have a physical address. Fortunately, some of our listed wonders are either located within a National Park or Reserve, or near a city, town, or place of business. For those that are not associated with a specific location, it is easiest to map it using GPS coordinates.

Luckily, Google has a system of codes that converts the coordinates into pin-drop locations that Google Maps can interpret and navigate.

Each adventure in this guide includes GPS coordinates along with a physical address whenever it is available.

It is important that you are prepared for poor cell signals. It is recommended that you route your location and ensure that the directions are accessible offline. Depending on your device and the distance of some locations, you may need to travel with a backup battery source.

About Wyoming

Wyoming received statehood in 1890, becoming the 44ᵗʰ state in the United States. Its capital city is Cheyenne, named after one of the prominent Native American tribes that inhabited the area as many as 12,000 years ago. The first European to arrive in what would eventually become Wyoming was explorer Francois Louis Verendrye, who traveled through the West in 1742. It wasn't until 1868 that Wyoming became a U.S. territory. Even then, Native Americans continued to battle for control of the land.

While experts aren't completely sure where Wyoming's name originated, there is ample evidence that it derives from a Native American word, possibly meaning "mountains and valleys alternating." It's also possible it came from the Munsee word that means "at the big river flat" or from the Algonquin term for "a large prairie place."

In 1869, Wyoming became the first state to grant women the right to vote, serve on juries, and hold public office, a full 51 years before the country followed suit. This remarkable achievement gives Wyoming its nickname, the Equality State, and its motto "Equal Rights."

Famous Americans from Wyoming include painter Jackson Pollock, actor Jim J. Bullock, children's book writer Patricia MacLachlan, musician Chris LeDoux, magician Tony Andruzzi, politician Harriet Elizabeth Byrd, politician Dick Cheney, politician Tom Coburn, U.S. Olympic gold medalist Rulon Gardner, the country's first female governor Nellie Tayloe Ross, entertainer William Frederick "Buffalo Bill" Cody, and physicist Robert R. Wilson.

Wyoming is the least populated state in the U.S., and 48 percent of the land is owned by the federal government. Its primary export is coal, as Wyoming is home to two of the largest coal mines in the world. Approximately 40 percent of the U.S. domestic supply of coal comes from Wyoming state mines.

Landscape and Climate

Bordered by Colorado and Utah in the south, Nebraska and South Dakota in the east, and Idaho and Utah in the west, Wyoming is one of just three states entirely bounded by straight lines. The state is divided into three distinct regions, which are the Great Plains in the east, the Rocky Mountains in the west, and the Intermontane Basins between the mountain ranges. Wyoming is home to the world's first national park, Yellowstone, and the first national monument, Devils Tower.

The Continental Divide splits Wyoming from the northwest corner to the southern border, and most water runoff drains into three major river systems: the Colorado, the Missouri, and the Columbia. Snow is common in the mountains, especially at higher elevations. The melt-off provides irrigation water for thousands of acres of land, generates electric power, and is put to use for domestic purposes.

Wyoming's climate is relatively cool, with the southern portion of the state having the highest temperatures, which vary between 85°F and 95°F in July. In winter, January temperatures can range as low as 5°F, but they typically average in the mid-30s for December, January, and February. Mountain elevations are usually colder, but even there, it is not uncommon to have long periods of mild weather with shorter cold spells.

Sunshine is frequent in Wyoming, with 75 percent sunny days in the summer and 60 percent in the winter. Mornings are generally clear, but clouds develop in the afternoon almost every day. There is very little fog or haze, which increases the intensity of the sun, particularly at high elevations.

More than 100 mammal species and 400 bird species call Wyoming home, including bison, wolves, grizzly bears, black bears, moose, elk, wild horses, mountain lions, pronghorn antelope, bald eagles, robins, woodpeckers, crows, doves, hummingbirds, orioles, falcons, and hawks.

Intermittent Spring

Also referred to as Periodic Spring, Intermittent Spring is the largest of only three rhythmic springs in the world. The theory behind why the spring doesn't flow constantly is that, as groundwater flows into the cavern, it fills a narrow tube that leads out of the cavern. Once the tube is filled, the water pours over the high point, creating a siphon effect and sucking the water out of the chamber. As the water empties the tube, air enters, breaking the siphon until the tube fills again. Although this is only speculation, a professor and hydrologist at the University of Utah stated, "We can't think of another explanation at the moment." The spring usually flows for about 18 straight minutes before stopping for another 18 minutes. Depending on the flow rate of the water, though, these times can vary.

Best Time to Visit: The Intermittent Spring flows best in late summer, so this would be the ideal time to visit.

Pass/Permit/Fees: There is no fee to visit.

Closest City or Town: Afton

Physical Address:
Star Valley Chamber of Commerce
360 Washington Street
Afton, WY 83110

GPS Coordinates: 42.74802° N, 110.84842° W

Did You Know? Intermittent Spring is said to have been discovered by the great-great-grandfather of Rulon Gardner, an Olympic gold medalist in Greco-Roman wrestling.

World's Largest Elkhorn Arch

Afton is home to the World's Largest Elkhorn Arch. As its name suggests, this attraction is a giant arch constructed entirely of elk antlers that passes over the four-lane highway of U.S. Route 89. The 75-foot-wide, 18-foot-tall arch comprises 3,011 intertwined elk antlers and weighs an estimated 15 tons. The Afton Chamber of Commerce planned the arch in 1956, and in July 1958, the Elkhorn Arch became a reality. The Wyoming Game and Fish Commission granted the Town of Afton a permit to gather naturally shed elk antlers in the National Elk Refuge, which is normally illegal. Antler-collection efforts continue annually to make repairs as necessary. In the early 2000s, the arch received another feature when a life-size wooden sculpture of two bull elk battling with their antlers was placed atop the arch. The sculpture was carved by Afton native Jonathan LaBenne.

Best Time to Visit: The World's Largest Elkhorn Arch is viewable at any time of the day or night.

Pass/Permit/Fees: There is no fee to visit the arch.

Closest City or Town: Afton

Physical Address:
458 Washington Street
Afton, WY 83110

GPS Coordinates: 42.72451° N, 110.93352° W

Did You Know? Built at a cost of $2,500 in 1958, the World's Largest Elkhorn Arch is now worth an estimated $300,000.

Devil's Gate

Devil's Gate, a natural rock formation that shows a split between two high cliffs, was a major landmark on both the Mormon and Oregon trails. While travelers heading west did not actually pass through the narrow opening, visitors today are able to hike a trail that runs through the cleft. The split between the two rock cliffs was created by the Sweetwater River; if the river had flowed just a kilometer to the south, it would have gone around the ridge instead of having to carve through it. Devil's Gate was a popular place for pioneers to stop on their way west to carve their names into the sides of the mountain. A trading post sprang up in the area in the early 1850s. It was abandoned in 1856 and partly burned that fall when two groups of travelers who'd waited too long to move on got caught in a snowstorm and needed the fire for warmth.

Best Time to Visit: The best time to visit Devil's Gate is in the spring, summer, or fall.

Pass/Permit/Fees: There is no fee to visit Devil's Gate.

Closest City or Town: Alcova

Physical Address:
Mormon Handcart Historic Site and Visitor Center
47600 W. Highway 220
Alcova, WY 82620

GPS Coordinates: 42.45087° N, 107.20982° W

Did You Know? Devil's Gate got its name from several murders that occurred in the region. As many as 20 people are buried near the gate.

Independence Rock

Independence Rock is a 130-foot-high granite rock in southwestern Natrona County. It was once a well-known landmark along the Mormon, Oregon, and California trails. Many of the 550,000 travelers who crossed the country using these trails carved their names into the rock. In addition to being tall, the rock is also long and wide, measuring 1,900 feet in length and 850 feet in width. From the top of the rock, you can see Devil's Gate, a 330-foot-deep ravine that cuts through the rock. When John C. Fremont camped near Independence Rock on August 1, 1843, he carved a large cross into the granite, but it was eventually blasted off on July 4, 1847 by pioneers. This was likely because many Protestants considered the cross a Catholic symbol and did not want it on the rock. Independence Rock was also the site of the first Masonic Lodge meeting in Wyoming.

Best Time to Visit: The best time to visit Independence Rock is in the spring, summer, or fall.

Pass/Permit/Fees: There is no fee to visit.

Closest City or Town: Alcova

Physical Address:
WY-220
Alcova, WY 82620

GPS Coordinates: 42.49374° N, 107.13181° W

Did You Know? One of the earliest names carved into Independence Rock is *M.K. Hugh*, dating back to 1824.

Grand Targhee Ski Resort

Grand Targhee Ski Resort offers some of the best snow in the world for skiing. Located in the Tetons, the resort receives over 500 inches of light powder snow each year and offers numerous trails to explore on skis, snowshoes, bikes, or foot. More than 600 acres are available for parties of up to 20 people who want to ski in the backcountry. A Snow Cat will take you and your guests to various remote skiing locations for a trip you'll never forget. Targhee is a great ski location for skiers and snowboarders who do not want to deal with crowds and ski lift lines. There are five lifts taking skiers and snowboarders up Fred's Mountain, Peaked Mountain, and Mary's Nipple. There are also close to 10 miles of groomed Nordic ski trails, over 6 miles of groomed fat-bike single-track trails, 8 miles of hiking-only trails, and numerous ski runs, the longest of which is the Teton Vista Traverse at 2.7 miles.

Best Time to Visit: While the resort is open year round, the best time to visit is during the winter for skiing.

Pass/Permit/Fees: Lift ticket prices start at $93 for adults, $42 for juniors, and $72 for seniors.

Closest City or Town: Alta

Physical Address:
3300 Ski Hill Road
Alta, WY 83414

GPS Coordinates: 43.78900° N, 110.95799° W

Did You Know? Grand Targhee Ski Resort has the best beginner ski terrain in Wyoming.

Crazy Woman Canyon

Located just outside of Bighorn National Forest, Crazy Woman Canyon features towering cliffs, a fast-moving creek, and some of the most stunning scenery in the state. This picturesque, lush canyon provided respite to weary travelers along the Bozeman Trail for decades, and the enormous rock walls offered the ideal hiding place for both Native American warriors and Western outlaws, no matter what or whom they were running from. Today, this canyon offers a nice change of pace from the more crowded outdoor attractions in the western part of Wyoming. Crazy Woman Canyon is usually not busy and is often entirely deserted. It provides an excellent trail for visitors who want to get away from the city.

Best Time to Visit: The best time to visit Crazy Woman Canyon is during the spring, summer, or fall.

Pass/Permit/Fees: There is no fee to visit.

Closest City or Town: Buffalo

Physical Address:
735 Crazy Woman Canyon Road
Buffalo, WY 82834

GPS Coordinates: 44.18675° N, 106.81025° W

Did You Know? Legend has it that Crazy Woman Canyon got its name from a woman who was traveling with her family via covered wagon when Sioux warriors attacked them, killing all but the woman. She reportedly lost her mind, stole an axe from a warrior, and killed four Sioux men before the remaining members fled.

Historic Occidental Hotel Museum

Take a trip back to the 1800s and early 1900s by visiting the Occidental Hotel Museum, a living history of the Old West. You'll see restored rooms and suites that have been returned to their original state, a saloon and restaurant, and the intricately etched windowpanes, all of which will give you a feeling of connectedness to the time when cowboys, Indians, cattle barons, outlaws, cattle rustlers, and lawmen lived among the high plains of Wyoming. Historical photographs, artifacts, and antiques tell the stories of the Bozeman Trail, local Indian battles, and the Johnson County Cattle War, just to name a few. The Occidental Hotel Museum is one of the last "Grand Old Hotels" of the West, and you can experience what it was like to relax in the lobby or grab a mug of root beer or sassafras in the authentic Western saloon. You can even see 23 bullet holes in the woodwork and tin ceiling from a time when gun battles were frequent.

Best Time to Visit: The hotel is open daily to the public.

Pass/Permit/Fees: There is no fee to visit, only to stay overnight. See the website for pricing details.

Closest City or Town: Buffalo

Physical Address:
10 N. Main Street
Buffalo, WY 82834

GPS Coordinates: 44.34720° N, 106.69938° W

Did You Know? The Historic Occidental Hotel is rumored to be haunted.

Ames Brothers Pyramid

Built by the Union Pacific Railroad in the early 1880s in an attempt to polish the rough reputation of Oliver and Oakes Ames, the Ames Brothers Pyramid was initially located near a remote railroad town to encourage passengers to disembark their train while the engines were changed.

Oliver and Oakes Ames used their wealth to take over the railroad. They then increased construction costs to illegally cheat taxpayers out of about $50 million. Oakes, a Massachusetts congressman, bribed his Washington counterparts to look the other way until the fraud was discovered in 1872. The pyramid was designed by noted architect Henry Hobson Richardson, and sculptor August St. Gaudens chiseled the portraits of Oliver and Oaks Ames into the pink granite near its peak.

Best Time to Visit: The pyramid is available to visit year round.

Pass/Permit/Fees: There is no fee to visit.

Closest City or Town: Buford

Physical Address:
211-205 Monument Road
Buford, WY 82052

GPS Coordinates: 41.13130° N, 105.39818° W

Did You Know? The portraits of the Ames brothers were positioned intentionally on the Ames Brothers Pyramid, with Oliver facing California and Oakes facing Washington, D.C.

Buford

Buford is a ghost town located between Laramie and Cheyenne along I-80. Buford's last resident, Don Sammons, who had been the only person living there for nearly 20 years, left the town in 2012. However, the sign announcing the town still says it has a population of one.

Buford was originally founded in 1866 as a military outpost while the Transcontinental Railroad was under construction nearby. A post office opened in Buford in 1900, and a school operated in the town between 1905 and 1962. Both services were eventually discontinued. Sammons and his family moved to Buford in 1980, and he was officer-in-charge of the post office until it closed. When Sammons decided to move in 2012, the town was auctioned off for $900,000 to Vietnamese buyer Pham Dinh Nguyen, who rebranded the town as PhinDeli Town Buford to advertise their PhinDeli imported Vietnamese coffee.

Best Time to Visit: Buford can be visited year round.

Pass/Permit/Fees: There is no fee to visit Buford.

Closest City or Town: Buford

Physical Address:
Buford Convenience Store/PhinDeli
2 Sammons Lane
Buford, WY 82052

GPS Coordinates: 41.12640° N, 105.30315° W

Did You Know? The PhinDeli Coffee venture failed, and the store was boarded up in 2017.

Tree in the Rock

The Tree in the Rock is a unique attraction in southeastern Wyoming that appears to be a tree growing out of a large, granite boulder. In a place where trees are rare, this sight is definitely eye-catching and a bit puzzling. The tree is actually growing out of a dirt-filled space between several big rocks, but the fact that it has survived in such a strange place makes it worth a stop as you drive through relatively treeless Wyoming on I-80.

The tree was discovered in 1867 when the Union Pacific was building its railroad in the area. The railroad workers were so astonished to see a tree growing there that they actually moved the planned tracks aside to make sure it was preserved. Eventually, the railroad was moved south and the road that runs past the tree was used first as a wagon trail and was later named the Lincoln Highway.

Best Time to Visit: The best time to visit the Tree in the Rock is during the day in the spring, summer, or fall.

Pass/Permit/Fees: There is no fee to visit.

Closest City or Town: Buford

Physical Address:
Laramie Area Visitor Center
800 S. 3rd Street
Laramie, WY 82070

GPS Coordinates: 41.13387° N, 105.34665° W

Did You Know? Lumber pines such as the Tree in the Rock can live up to 2,000 years.

16

Alcova Reservoir

At 2,470 acres in size, Alcova Reservoir is the main recreation area serving Casper and the surrounding region. The two most popular activities in the summer are water skiing and sail boating, and in the winter, ice fishing attracts visitors from all over the state. Boat and bike rentals are available at the onsite marina, Alcova Reservoir, which also features a restaurant, ice cream parlor, convenience stores, and a fuel dock. Visitors may also want to explore the Cottonwood Creek Dinosaur Trail, an interpretive trail that takes guests on a journey through various geological eras. It is located near Cottonwood Creek Beach on the shores of the reservoir.

Best Time to Visit: Alcova Reservoir is open year round, but Alcova Resort is only open between May 15 and September 15 from 8:00 a.m. to 8:00 p.m.

Pass/Permit/Fees: There is no fee to visit unless you intend to camp overnight. Visit the website for details.

Closest City or Town: Casper

Physical Address:
Casper Area Convention & Visitors Bureau
139 W. 2nd Street, Suite 1B
Casper, WY 82601

GPS Coordinates: 42.52974° N, 106.76596° W

Did You Know? Alcova Dam, which created Alcova Reservoir, was completed between 1935 and 1937. It provides both irrigation and hydroelectric power.

Bar Nunn

Bar Nunn is a town in Wyoming that sits on the former site of Wardwell Field, the airport that served Natron County until 1952. Romie Nunn, a well-known businessman and rancher, owned some of the Wardwell Field Property and purchased the rest of it when the airport relocated to land along U.S. Highway 20-26. Nunn wanted his expanded property to become "the horse center of the Rockies," but he eventually subdivided it in 1958 and named it the Bar Nunn Ranch Subdivision. The subdivision found it increasingly difficult to receive services such as snow removal and street repairs, so in 1982, it became a town, allowing it to improve services to its residents and gain new funding paths.

Best Time to Visit: The best time to visit Bar Nunn is June, August, or September.

Pass/Permit/Fees: There is no fee to visit Bar Nunn.

Closest City or Town: Casper

Physical Address:
Town of Bar Nunn
4820 N. Wardwell Industrial Avenue
Bar Nunn, WY 82601

GPS Coordinates: 42.91648° N, 106.34034° W

Did You Know? The runways of the former airport that is now Bar Nunn serve as the town's streets.

Casper

The second-largest city in Wyoming, Casper has a rich history in oil production and as a primary location along the Oregon and Mormon trails. It was also the site of a fort that was built during the 19th century to protect mail and telegraph service throughout the "Wild West," particularly when Native American attacks increased following the 1864 Sand Creek Massacre in Colorado. Casper wasn't founded until after the fort closed. Crude oil was discovered in the 1890s, making Casper the center of the regional petroleum industry. Today, Casper is home to top-notch outdoor recreational opportunities such as hiking, fishing, skiing, rock climbing, biking, snowshoeing, and more. In terms of historical importance, Casper is the only place in the country where the Mormon, Oregon, California, and Pony Express trails intersected.

Best Time to Visit: Casper is excellent to visit year round.

Pass/Permit/Fees: There is no fee to visit Casper.

Closest City or Town: Casper

Physical Address:
Casper Area Convention & Visitor Bureau
139 W. 2nd Street, Suite 1B
Casper, WY 82601

GPS Coordinates: 42.84875° N, 106.32643° W

Did You Know? The fort that was built on what is now Casper was named "Fort Caspar," but due to a typo when the town's name was officially registered, it was spelled with an *e* instead of an *a*.

Hell's Half Acre

Hell's Half Acre is a unique geological formation about 40 miles west of Casper. It spans 960 acres and is comprised of caves, ravines, and oddly shaped rock formations. Native American tribes once used the deep ravines in the area to drive thousands of buffalo to their deaths, forcing them to jump over the cliffs during their hunts. At various times during the past, the site was named "The Devil's Kitchen," "The Baby Grand Canyon," and "The Pits of Hades," but when a cowhand called it "Hell's Half Acre," the name became part of an advertising campaign designed to bring visitors to Casper to see the roadside attraction. There is no public access to the valley itself, but visitors can drive to a large gravel lot to get a close view of the strange topography. There is also an interpretive sign at the location that provides information about the history of the area.

Best Time to Visit: Hell's Half Acre can be viewed at any time of the year.

Pass/Permit/Fees: There is no fee to visit Hell's Half Acre.

Closest City or Town: Casper

Physical Address:
Casper Area Convention & Visitors Bureau
139 W. 2nd Street, Suite 1B
Casper, WY 82601

GPS Coordinates: 43.03990° N, 107.09346° W

Did You Know? Hell's Half Acre was the setting for the fictional planet of Klendathu in the film *Starship Troopers*.

National Historic Trails Interpretive Center

The National Historic Trails Interpretive Center provides information related to the state as well as interactive exhibits on the Oregon, Mormon, Pony Express, and California trails, all of which passed through the area between 1841 and 1868. The hands-on experiences at the center allow visitors to understand the lives of the more than 400,000 pioneers who came through Wyoming on these trails for more than 20 years. In addition to permanent exhibits, on the weekends, you'll find even more programs available, such as *Meek's Cutoff*, *Voices of Independence Rock*, *Let's Follow the Trail – County Roads 308/319*, *Artifact Road Show*, and others.

Best Time to Visit: The National Historic Trails Interpretive Center is open daily between 9:00 a.m. to 4:30 p.m.

Pass/Permit/Fees: There is no fee to visit the center.

Closest City or Town: Casper

Physical Address:
1501 N. Poplar Street
Casper, WY 82601

GPS Coordinates: 42.86648° W. 106.33719° W

Did You Know? The National Historic Trails Interpretive Center opened to the public in 2002 as a partnership between the Bureau of Land Management, the National Historic Trails Center Foundation, and the city of Casper.

North Platte River

The North Platte River is a recreational waterway located in central Wyoming. It is the only floatable river in this part of the state, and it has become a world-class fishing destination for brown, cutthroat, and rainbow trout. In addition to floating and fishing, other popular recreational activities on the North Platte include waterfowl hunting, camping, picnicking, and wildlife observation.

The North Platte River is a tributary of the Platte River, and it runs for about 716 miles through Wyoming, Colorado, and Nebraska before it joins the South Platte River to from the Platte River. The North Platte has been a vital westward route, providing water and grass for animals and travelers.

Best Time to Visit: The best time to visit the North Platte River for fishing is between mid-June and early August. The summer is best for floating and camping.

Pass/Permit/Fees: There is no fee to visit.

Closest City or Town: Casper

Physical Address:
Casper Area Convention & Visitors Bureau
139 W. 2nd Street, Suite 1B
Casper, WY 82601

GPS Coordinates: 41.36949° N, 106.70713° W

Did You Know? In 1847, several ferries operated out of Casper that offered passage across the North Platte River.

Cheyenne

Cheyenne, the state's capital, was established in 1867 as the mountain-region headquarters of the Union Pacific Railroad. Initially, a U.S. Army site named Fort D. A. Russell was designed to protect the railroad. However, Cheyenne's population grew so quickly that it earned the nickname of the "Magic City of the Plains."

Today, Cheyenne is known as the quintessential cowboy town. The flavor of the Old West is still prominent, particularly in its annual hosting of the Cheyenne Frontier Days rodeo and festival, a 10-day event held the last week in July that boasts the largest outdoor rodeo in the country. Cheyenne Frontier Days is known as the world's largest Western celebration, or the "Daddy of 'Em All," and draws in over 260,000 participants each year.

Best Time to Visit: The best time to visit Cheyenne is during Cheyenne Frontier Days in July.

Pass/Permit/Fees: There is no fee to visit Cheyenne.

Closest City or Town: Cheyenne

Physical Address:
Visit Cheyenne
121 W. 15th Street
Cheyenne, WY 82001

GPS Coordinates: 41.13189° N, 104.81464° W

Did You Know? Cheyenne was named for the Cheyenne Native American tribe that lived in the area in the 1800s. The word *Cheyenne* means "people of the strange tongue."

Cheyenne Botanic Gardens

At the Cheyenne Botanic Gardens, visitors will be enchanted by the incredible displays of award-winning plants, trees, and shrubs from all over the world. Perennial and annual flowers add color to the dazzling landscapes, and a vegetable garden brings attention to delicious foods that can grow in the Wyoming climate. Exhibits at the Cheyenne Botanic Gardens include the xeriscape garden, the Bedont Rose Garden, the Reckling Herb Garden, the cacti garden, the wetland garden, the Cottage Garden, and the woodland garden, among other attractions. Educational opportunities for children and adults are available weekly and include topics such as *Bee Keeping Basics*, *Dirt! Foundations of Soil*, *Meet the Birds*, and *All Things Tulips*, among others.

Best Time to Visit: The Cheyenne Botanic Gardens is open year round Tuesday through Saturday from 10:00 a.m. to 5:00 p.m. and on Sundays in June, July, and August from 12:00 p.m. to 5:00 p.m.

Pass/Permit/Fees: There is no fee to visit the gardens.

Closest City or Town: Cheyenne

Physical Address:
710 S. Lions Park Drive
Cheyenne, WY 82001

GPS Coordinates: 41.15593° N, 104.83052° W

Did You Know? The Grand Conservatory at the Cheyenne Botanic Gardens features a 34-foot-tall palm tree, a bonsai house, and a Baroque-style orangerie.

Cheyenne Frontier Days Rodeo

Every year in July, Cheyenne is host to the world's largest outdoor rodeo, known the world over as the Cheyenne Frontier Days Rodeo. It first debuted in 1897, and today, the 10-day event is much more than just a rodeo. Not only is there bull riding, bronc riding, steer wrestling, calf roping, and barrel racing, but there's also nightly music concerts that feature some of the biggest stars in country and rock music. Don't forget to attend the Grand Parade, which is held Tuesday, Thursday, and both Saturdays of the festival. The parade showcases marching bands, floats, antique carriages, horses, automobiles, and characters in period dress. A carnival also runs near the rodeo grounds from 10:30 a.m. to midnight every day and features rides, games, and Wild West activities.

Best Time to Visit: Cheyenne Frontier Days occurs annually the last week of July and runs for 10 days.

Pass/Permit/Fees: There is no fee to visit the Cheyenne Frontier Days Rodeo parade, but there is a cost for all other activities. Exact pricing varies based on event selection, age of the participant, seat selection, and date selection.

Closest City or Town: Cheyenne

Physical Address:
1230 W. 8th Avenue
Cheyenne, WY 82001

GPS Coordinates: 41.15820° N, 104.83395° W

Did You Know? Cheyenne Frontier Days was inducted into the ProRodeo Hall of Fame in 2008.

Chugwater Soda Fountain

The Chugwater Soda Fountain is the oldest soda fountain still in operation in the state and the longest continually running business in Chugwater itself. It has been in operation for more than 100 years, and while it was originally part of a drugstore and general store, the soda fountain is now a full-service restaurant. The building that houses the soda fountain was built in 1914 and rebuilt in 1916 after a fire partially destroyed the structure. The soda fountain's bar was initially installed in Rock Creek, but when the railroad arrived in 1927, the owner sold his equipment to the Chugwater drugstore. The bar had to be broken into three pieces so that it could be packed in wagons and transported through the mountains for reassembly and installation in Chugwater.

Best Time to Visit: The Chugwater Soda Fountain is open Monday through Saturday from 8:00 a.m. to 5:00 p.m. and Sunday from 9:00 a.m. to 5:00 p.m.

Pass/Permit/Fees: There is no fee to visit the Chugwater Soda Fountain, but you will need money for sodas.

Closest City or Town: Cheyenne

Physical Address:
314 1st Street
Chugwater, WY 82210

GPS Coordinates: 41.75695° N, 104.82142° W

Did You Know? The stuffed elk overlooking the Chugwater Soda Fountain is named Wendell. He has resided in the building since 1947.

Curt Gowdy State Park

This 3,395-acre public park is located halfway between Cheyenne and Laramie. It is well-known for its extensive trail system, fishing spots, and Hynds Lodge, a conference and accommodation space built by Harry P. Hynds in 1922. Visitors can rent out the lodge, which can accommodate up to 30 people for overnight stays or 90 people for parties, meetings, and other events. There is also a large kitchen, dining room, living room, stone fireplace, and covered porch in the lodge as well. Curt Gowdy State Park offers more than 35 miles of trails for hiking, biking, and horseback riding. Fish that can be caught in the three park reservoirs include perch, brown trout, lake trout, rainbow trout, and kokanee salmon.

Best Time to Visit: Visit in the spring, summer, or fall.

Pass/Permit/Fees: The fee to visit Curt Gowdy State Park is $6 for residents and $9 for nonresidents per vehicle.

Closest City or Town: Cheyenne

Physical Address:
1264 Granite Springs Road
Cheyenne, WY 82009

GPS Coordinates: 41.16951° N, 105.22803° W

Did You Know? Curt Gowdy State Park was originally called Granite State Park, but it was renamed to honor Wyoming native Curt Gowdy in 1972. Gowdy was a two-sport varsity athlete in basketball and tennis at the University of Wyoming in Laramie and a noted sportscaster and outdoorsman.

Quebec 01 Missile Alert Facility

The Quebec 01 Missile Alert Facility is a former military installation that controlled a nuclear weapon designed and built by the United States. It is the only accessible such facility left in the world, and it's committed to preserving and interpreting the history of the Cold War in the late 20th century. The Quebec 01 Missile Alert Facility was built in 1962 as a Minuteman I Launch Control Center, but it was upgraded to a missile-alert facility in 1986. Today, visitors can descend 50 feet into the capsule and tour the location of one of the most powerful weapons the U.S. has ever designed.

Best Time to Visit: The facility is open daily from May 1 to September 30 from 9:00 a.m. to 5:00 p.m.

Pass/Permit/Fees: The fee to visit the Quebec 01 Missile Alert Facility is $8 for adults, $7 for military members, and $4 for children between the ages of 12 and 17. Children ages 11 and under are free.

Closest City or Town: Cheyenne

Physical Address:
Visit Cheyenne
121 W. 15th Street
Cheyenne, WY 82001

GPS Coordinates: 41.54331° N, 104.90262° W

Did You Know? The Quebec 01 Missile Alert Facility, and all other Peacekeeper Missile Alert Facilities, was decommissioned in 2005 to comply with the Strategic Offensive Reductions Treaty (SORT).

Artist Point

Artist Point, one of the most famous overlooks in Yellowstone National Park, provides visitors with a spectacular view of the 308-foot Lower Falls. The viewpoint sticks out from the Grand Canyon's south wall and is short walk from South Rim Drive. You're certain to recognize the view, as it is arguably the most photographed area in the national park. Lower Falls is in the deep, V-shaped rocks and sends between 5,000 and 60,000 gallons of water over the ledge every second. The volume of water depends on the season, with the spring and early summer boasting the highest amount. Straight down from Artist Point is a 1,000-foot-deep chasm, and the north rim of the canyon is just 0.75 miles from the overlook.

Best Time to Visit: The best time to visit Artist Point is in the spring to catch the waterfall at its fullest.

Pass/Permit/Fees: There is a $35 fee for a 7-day pass to enter Yellowstone National Park and visit Artist Point.

Closest City or Town: Cody

Physical Address:
Cody Chamber of Commerce & Visitor Center
836 Sheridan Avenue
Cody, Wyoming 82414

GPS Coordinates: 44.72434° N, 110.47920° W

Did You Know? Artist Point got its name from the location where artist Thomas Moran gained inspiration for his oil paintings *The Grand Canyon of the Yellowstone* and *Lower Falls, Yellowstone Park* in 1871.

Beartooth Mountains

Located in northwest Wyoming, the Beartooth Mountains are part of the Greater Yellowstone Ecosystem because of their proximity to Yellowstone National Park. Until the 1870s, Beartooth Mountain was used by the Crow Tribe as hunting grounds and winter shelter, where they were shielded from the harsh winds of the plains. Trappers entered the area in the 1830s, and the U.S. government began formal exploration in 1878 with the aim of expanding mining operations. However, the remoteness of the mountains limited the amount of mining products that came from the mines that eventually cropped up.

There are more than 34,000 square miles of intact or nearly intact wilderness in the Beartooth Mountains, providing necessary habitat protection for grizzly bears, mountain lions, lynx, wolverines, bison, elk, and wolves.

Best Time to Visit: The best time to visit the Beartooth Mountains is in the spring, summer, or fall.

Pass/Permit/Fees: There is no fee to visit the area.

Closest City or Town: Cody

Physical Address:
Cody Chamber of Commerce & Visitor Center
836 Sheridan Avenue
Cody, Wyoming 82414

GPS Coordinates: 45.24039° N, 109.79299° W

Did You Know? The highest peak in the Beartooth Mountains is Granite Peak at 12,807 feet.

Biscuit Basin

Biscuit Basin is a thermal basin located in Yellowstone National Park's Upper Geyser Basin. It features the Biscuit Basin Loop, a 0.66-mile hike that takes visitors past various hot springs and active geysers. While the hydrothermal features in the Biscuit Basin will probably be calm during most visits, it does sit in a particularly volatile geologic area, so stay on the boardwalk when hiking the loop. Thermal ground can be extremely hot. The geysers and springs include the Black Opal Pool, the Jewel Geyser, the Sapphire Pool, the Black Pearl Geyser, Shell Spring, Mustard Spring, and Avoca Spring.

Best Time to Visit: The best time to visit the Biscuit Basin is during April, September, or October when the crowds are thinner.

Pass/Permit/Fees: There is a $35 fee for a 7-day pass to enter Yellowstone National Park and visit the basin.

Closest City or Town: Cody

Physical Address:
Cody Chamber of Commerce & Visitor Center
836 Sheridan Avenue
Cody, Wyoming 82414

GPS Coordinates: 44.48571° N, 110.85641° W

Did You Know? Biscuit Basin got its name when a 1959 earthquake that registered 7.5 on the Richter scale caused the Sapphire Pool to violently erupt and send "rock biscuits" around the area.

Buffalo Bill Dam

The Buffalo Bill Dam was built between 1905 and 1910 at the behest of William "Buffalo Bill" Cody, who wanted to create a reservoir to irrigate the Bighorn Basin and turn it into productive agricultural land. At the time it was completed, the Buffalo Bill Dam was the largest dam in the world. It was part of the Shoshone Project, which included several plans to turn the semi-arid plains of Wyoming into land that could grow crops.

The dam, which features a concrete arch-gravity design, is 70 feet wide at its base and 200 feet wide at its crest. The construction of the dam was fraught with problems, including workers' deaths, floods, and labor strikes. Even after it was completed, it still encountered issues like leaks and reduced capacity due to a heavy silt load.

Best Time to Visit: The best time to visit the Buffalo Bill Dam is in the spring, summer, or fall.

Pass/Permit/Fees: There is no fee to visit the dam.

Closest City or Town: Cody

Physical Address:
Buffalo Bill Dam & Visitor Center
4808 N. Fork Highway
Cody, WY 82414

GPS Coordinates: 44.50155° N, 109.18393° W

Did You Know? The Buffalo Bill Dam was originally named the Shoshone Dam but was renamed to honor visionary William "Buffalo Bill" Cody in 1946.

Continental Divide Trail

Approximately 550 miles of the 3,100-mile-long Continental Divide Trail pass through Wyoming, beginning in Yellowstone National Park and ending in the Snowy Range in Medicine Bow National Forest. It passes through some of the most spectacular wilderness in the country. In addition to hiking this trail, there are plenty of other activities to participate in as well, including fishing and snowshoeing.

The Continental Divide Trail is segmented into eight parts in Wyoming: Old Faithful, Teton Wilderness, Gros Ventre, Bridger Wilderness, Sweetwater River, Great Divide Basin, Ferrir Mountains, and Sierra Madre.

Best Time to Visit: The best time to visit the trail in Wyoming is during the spring, summer, or fall.

Pass/Permit/Fees: While there is no fee to hike the Continental Divide Trail, there are fees for various national parks and forests that the trail passes through.

Closest City or Town: Cody

Physical Address:
Cody Country Chamber of Commerce Visitor Center
836 Sheridan Avenue
Cody, WY 82414

GPS Coordinates: 42.68435° N, 109.13934° W

Did You Know? The Great Divide Basin on the Continental Divide Trail is the only place where the trail splits and then rejoins.

Dragon's Mouth Springs

Located in Yellowstone National Park, Dragon's Mouth Springs is a hot spring that flows out of a deep cave. The steam that is produced when the hot water hits the cold air makes it appear to be smoke from the mouth of a dragon. Additionally, the hot water releases gasses and steam inside the cave, creating pressure bubbles that pop against the cave's ceiling. When this occurs, a booming and gurgling sound can be heard throughout the cave and the area surrounding it. The sound resembles a growling dragon that might be getting ready to torch anyone who is unfortunate enough to be nearby. In Native American legends, the steaming cave was interpreted as an angry bull bison and the sounds as the animal's snorts. Dragon's Mouth is located in the center of Yellowstone National Park, closest to the east entrance in Wyoming.

Best Time to Visit: Visit during the spring and fall.

Pass/Permit/Fees: There is a $35 fee for a 7-day pass to enter Yellowstone National Park and visit the springs.

Closest City or Town: Cody

Physical Address:
Cody Country Chamber of Commerce Visitor Center
836 Sheridan Avenue
Cody, WY 82414

GPS Coordinates: 44.62934° N, 110.43621° W

Did You Know? The temperature of the water coming from Dragon's Mouth Springs is 170.2°F, so it is important to stay on the boardwalk to avoid burns.

Fairy Falls

With its 220-foot-high plunge-style stream, Fairy Falls is the largest front-country waterfall in Yellowstone National Park. While it is a narrow fall, it is consistent throughout the year, even with little rain. If you look at the waterfall closely, you may see that there is actually a waterfall behind the main waterfall caused by some seepage from the rocks in the middle.

The hike to the falls is a 4.1-mile point-to-point journey that is rated as easy because it is flat and well-defined. There is a slight incline to the falls, but it's not steep and can be easily navigated by hikers of all abilities. The trail to Fairy Falls joins routes leading to the Grand Prismatic Spring and the Imperial and Spray geysers.

Best Time to Visit: The best time to visit Fairy Falls is in the spring, summer, or fall.

Pass/Permit/Fees: There is a $35 fee for a 7-day pass to enter Yellowstone National Park and visit the falls.

Closest City or Town: Cody

Physical Address:
Cody Country Chamber of Commerce Visitor Center
836 Sheridan Avenue
Cody, WY 82414

GPS Coordinates: 44.52739° N, 110.87064° W

Did You Know? Geologists also note that Fairy Creek, which is responsible for Fairy Falls, is likely in the beginning stages of carving out a natural rock bridge.

Firehole River

Firehole River is one of two major Madison River tributaries in northwestern Wyoming. It is part of the Missouri River system and flows through several geyser basins in Yellowstone National Park. The Firehole River is the source of three major waterfalls and is a popular fishing destination for serious fly fishermen. Even though the river contains high levels of boron and arsenic, brown trout are abundant, having first been introduced to the river in 1890. Today, all stocking programs have been discontinued, so all trout pulled from the Firehole River are wild. The river's water is warm (as high as 86°F) due to the surrounding geothermal influence of the various geysers, springs, and other features in Yellowstone.

Best Time to Visit: The best time to visit Firehole River is in June, especially for fishing.

Pass/Permit/Fees: There is a $35 fee for a 7-day pass to enter Yellowstone National Park and visit the river.

Closest City or Town: Cody

Physical Address:
Cody Country Chamber of Commerce Visitor Center
836 Sheridan Avenue
Cody, WY 82414

GPS Coordinates: 44.59347° N, 110.83142° W

Did You Know? The Firehole River got its name from early trappers who thought the steam rising from it resembled smoke from a fire.

Gibbon Falls

Located in Yellowstone National Park, Gibbon Falls is a waterfall that gradually drops about 84 feet along the Gibbon River. You can park near the top of the falls and have a wonderful view of the rushing water, but you'll probably need to wait your turn to see it because this viewing area can get crowded. You can also follow the paved trail from the viewing area above the river to find a spot where you can see the falls without the crowd. The large cascade is split into two flows by a band of rock in the middle. On the right side, when the river flows across a ledge, it shoots the water into the air, creating a rooster-tail effect. The cliff over which the river flows is the remnant of the Yellowstone caldera rim, which was created by a large volcanic eruption about 640,000 years ago.

Best Time to Visit: The best time to visit Gibbon Falls is in the spring or summer after a heavy rain.

Pass/Permit/Fees: There is a $35 fee for a 7-day pass to enter Yellowstone National Park and visit Gibbons Falls.

Closest City or Town: Cody

Physical Address:
Cody Country Chamber of Commerce Visitor Center
836 Sheridan Avenue
Cody, WY 82414

GPS Coordinates: 44.65422° N, 110.77091° W

Did You Know? Gibbon Falls was discovered in 1872 by William Henry Jackson and John Merle Coulter of the second Hayden Survey.

Grand Prismatic Spring

The Grand Prismatic Spring is the most photographed thermal feature in Yellowstone National Park and is located halfway between the Upper and Lower Geyser basins. Its huge size and the bright rings of green, yellow, and orange surrounding the deep blue water make it a spectacular sight to see. The colors come from various species of thermophile bacteria that live in the progressively cooler water the further they get from the center of the hot springs. In the summer, the colors tend to feature more oranges and reds, while in the winter, they appear dark green. Due to the extreme heat in the center of the spring, the water in the middle, where it reaches a depth of 160 feet, is completely sterile. The Grand Prismatic Spring is the third-largest spring in the world and the largest one in the U.S.

Best Time to Visit: The best time to visit is during the summer to see the most variation of colors.

Pass/Permit/Fees: There is a $35 fee for a 7-day pass to enter Yellowstone National Park and visit the spring.

Closest City or Town: Cody

Physical Address:
Cody Country Chamber of Commerce Visitor Center
836 Sheridan Avenue
Cody, WY 82414

GPS Coordinates: 44.52529° N, 110.83824° W

Did You Know? In 2014, a tourist from the Netherlands accidentally flew a drone into the Grand Prismatic Spring. It disappeared and has never resurfaced.

Hayden Valley

When you wish to see wildlife, head over to Hayden Valley where the animals congregate. As you make your way through the valley, you'll see herds of bison, elk, and every once in a while, a grizzly bear. There are plenty of ducks, pelicans, and Canadian geese gathered around the Yellowstone River. Along the road through the valley, there are several roadside scenic turnouts. These panoramic views allow you to see any wildlife that enters the sparsely covered ground. The valley was once part of Yellowstone Lake and contains glacial till left over from the most recent glacial retreat, which was 13,000 years ago. Glacial till is made up of numerous soils, including clay, which prevents the ground from readily absorbing water, keeping the ground marshy and mostly free of trees.

Best Time to Visit: The best time to visit Hayden Valley is in the spring or summer when wildlife is more active.

Pass/Permit/Fees: There is a $35 fee for a 7-day pass to enter Yellowstone National Park and visit the valley.

Closest City or Town: Cody

Physical Address:
Cody Country Chamber of Commerce Visitor Center
836 Sheridan Avenue
Cody, WY 82414

GPS Coordinates: 44.64675° N, 110.45582° W

Did You Know? Hayden Valley is named for Ferdinand Vandeveer Hayden, whose surveys led to the creation of Yellowstone National Park.

Isa Lake

Straddling the Continental Divide at Craig Pass in Yellowstone National Park, Isa Lake is also known as Two-Ocean Lake because it's one of just a few natural lakes in the world that drain into two different oceans. The east side of Isa Lake drains into the Pacific Ocean by way of the Lewis River, and the west side drains into the Gulf of Mexico by way of the Firehole River. However, it only does this at the peak of snow melt following winters with deep snowfall. At other times of the year, there isn't enough precipitation to allow the lake to drain in both directions. Isa Lake is well-known for its thriving population of great yellow pond lilies, which are easily recognized by their large floating green leaves and bright yellow blooms.

Best Time to Visit: Visit Isa Lake during the spring after a winter that experienced heavy snowfall.

Pass/Permit/Fees: There is a $35 fee for a 7-day pass to enter Yellowstone National Park and visit Isa Lake.

Closest City or Town: Cody

Physical Address:
Cody Country Chamber of Commerce Visitor Center
836 Sheridan Avenue
Cody, WY 82414

GPS Coordinates: 44.44198° N, 110.71875° W

Did You Know? Hirram M. Chittenden, an American engineer and historian, named the lake for Miss Isabel Jelke, but the reason for this honor is not clear.

Lone Star Geyser

This incredible geyser in Yellowstone National Park boasts a 12-foot-high cone (base) and a 50-foot-high burst of water. It erupts predictably every 3 hours or so and provides visitors with a performance that can last up to 30 minutes in length. The major eruption is usually preceded by several smaller eruptions and periods of no movement at all. Visitors to the area should remain for up to an hour to be sure they get to see the main event. There is a logbook at the site for visitors to record each eruption so that subsequent guests can better predict when the Lone Star Geyser is set to erupt again. The trail to the Lone Star Geyser is 2.5 miles from the Grand Loop Road, about 2 miles south of Old Faithful Village. The trailhead is just upstream from the Kepler Cascades.

Best Time to Visit: Visit in the spring, summer, or fall.

Pass/Permit/Fees: There is a $35 fee for a 7-day pass to enter Yellowstone National Park and visit the geyser.

Closest City or Town: Cody

Physical Address:
Cody Country Chamber of Commerce Visitor Center
836 Sheridan Avenue
Cody, WY 82414

GPS Coordinates: 44.42149° N, 110.80735° W

Did You Know? At first, the Lone Star Geyser was thought to be the only one in the area, giving it its name. But since then, 11 more geysers have been identified in this isolated section of Yellowstone.

Mammoth Hot Springs

Located just south of Yellowstone National Park's north entrance is a must-see feature called Mammoth Hot Springs. The reason the Mammoth Hot Springs are unique is because they don't look anything like the other thermal features in the park due to being surrounded by limestone. The limestone allows the travertine formations to grow more quickly than elsewhere, making it look like a "cave turned inside out." The hot water coming up from the underground molten-magma chamber dissolves the limestone on its way to the surface, but when it is exposed to air, the dissolved limestone reforms into its solid state, creating the awesome formations around the springs.

Best Time to Visit: The best time to visit Mammoth Hot Spring is in the spring, summer, or fall, but the area is accessible by car year round.

Pass/Permit/Fees: There is a $35 fee for a 7-day pass to enter Yellowstone National Park and visit the springs.

Closest City or Town: Cody

Physical Address:
Cody Country Chamber of Commerce Visitor Center
836 Sheridan Avenue
Cody, WY 82414

GPS Coordinates: 44.97954° N, 110.70050° W

Did You Know? At Mammoth Hot Springs, there are several sinkholes on the parade ground, which gave developers of the Mammoth Hotel and Fort Yellowstone concern that it would not support the structures.

Morning Glory Pool

Morning Glory Pool, also referred to as Morning Glory Spring, is a hot spring located in Yellowstone National Park's Upper Geyser Basin. The center of the formation is a bright blue, which is due to the bacteria that inhabit the water. At one time, only the edges of the pool were yellow and orange, but these colors have been gradually creeping toward the center as the spring's temperature has decreased over time. In 1883, Morning Glory Pool was given its name by the wife of Assistant Park Superintendent Charles McGowan. She thought the pool looked like the morning glory flower. Morning Glory Pool rarely erupts as a geyser but may do so following an earthquake.

Best Time to Visit: The best time to visit Morning Glory Pool is in the spring, summer, or fall.

Pass/Permit/Fees: There is a $35 fee for a 7-day pass to enter Yellowstone National Park and visit the pool.

Closest City or Town: Cody

Physical Address:
Cody Country Chamber of Commerce Visitor Center
836 Sheridan Avenue
Cody, WY 82414

GPS Coordinates: 44.47689° N, 110.84365° W

Did You Know? Mrs. McGowan actually called the feature *Convolutus*, which is the Latin name for the morning glory flower, but by 1889, everyone was using the English name.

Mount Washburn

Mount Washburn is a 10,219-foot peak in the Washburn Mountains that overlooks the northern portion of Yellowstone National Park. The incredible panoramic views of Yellowstone that are only present on Mount Washburn make it one of the most popular places for summer hikes in the state. One of three lookout towers in Yellowstone is located on Mount Washburn's summit, which also includes a small visitor center and restrooms. Additionally, on clear days, visitors can even see the Teton Mountain Range. Mount Washburn Trail is the most popular hike of the two trails that lead to the top, climbing 1,400 feet by way of moderate switchbacks. There is plenty to see on the trek up to the summit, including diverse flora and open views of Yellowstone.

Best Time to Visit: The best time to visit Mount Washburn is in the spring or fall to avoid crowds.

Pass/Permit/Fees: There is a $35 fee for a 7-day pass to enter Yellowstone National Park and view the site.

Closest City or Town: Cody

Physical Address:
Cody Country Chamber of Commerce Visitor Center
836 Sheridan Avenue
Cody, WY 82414

GPS Coordinates: 44.79990° N, 110.43368° W

Did You Know? Mount Washburn is named for Henry Washburn of the 1870 Washburn-Langford-Doane expedition.

44

Mystic Falls Trail

The 2.4-mile hike to Mystic Falls is a there-and-back trail that starts and ends at the Biscuit Basin Trailhead, located approximately 3 miles north of Old Faithful. It follows a nicely flowing creek through a mixed conifer forest and ends at the Mystic Falls waterfall. This waterfall is a 70-foot drop of the Little Firehole River, which flows from the Madison Plateau above. Once you reach the falls, you can either turn around and head back, or you can climb the switchbacks another 500 feet to an overlook of the Upper Geyser Basin. This adds about 1.5 miles to the hike since you'll loop back to the main trail from the overlook. The route also passes several thermal features on your way to Mystic Falls, including the Sapphire Pool and Jewel Geyser.

Best Time to Visit: The best time to visit the Mystic Falls Trail is between May and October.

Pass/Permit/Fees: There is a $35 fee for a 7-day pass to enter Yellowstone National Park and visit the trail.

Closest City or Town: Cody

Physical Address:
Cody Country Chamber of Commerce Visitor Center
836 Sheridan Avenue
Cody, WY 82414

GPS Coordinates: 44.48446° N, 110.86886° W

Did You Know? Mystic Falls was originally named Little Firehole Falls but was changed in 1885 by members of the Arnold Hague Geological Survey.

Norris Geyser Basin

Of all the thermal areas in Yellowstone National Park, the Norris Geyser Basin is the oldest, hottest, and most dynamic. Norris has had thermal features for at least 115,000 years, and they change daily due to the frequent seismic disturbances and water fluctuations. The thermal features in this basin are also acidic, which is rare in Yellowstone. There are two areas in the Norris Geyser Basin: the Back Basin and the Porcelain Basin. The Back Basin is heavily wooded and has thermal features scattered throughout the area, which can be viewed from a 1.5-mile boardwalk that encircles it. The Porcelain Basin has no trees and offers a complete sensory experience in color, smell, and sound. Visitors can access this area by way of a 0.75-mile boardwalk and natural trail.

Best Time to Visit: The best time to visit the Norris Geyser Basin is in spring, summer, or fall.

Pass/Permit/Fees: There is a $35 fee for a 7-day pass to enter Yellowstone National Park and visit the basin.

Closest City or Town: Cody

Physical Address:
Cody Country Chamber of Commerce Visitor Center
836 Sheridan Avenue
Cody, WY 82414

GPS Coordinates: 44.72830° N, 110.70394° W

Did You Know? The hottest water temperature ever recorded in Yellowstone was in the Norris Geyser Basin, measuring 459°F at 1,087 feet below the surface.

Old Faithful Geyser

The most famous geyser in Yellowstone National Park, the Old Faithful Geyser is so named for its regular and frequent water eruptions. In fact, Old Faithful has erupted more than a million times since Yellowstone was designated the first national park in 1872. Located in Yellowstone's Upper Geyser Basin, there is an easily accessible viewing area that includes bench seating, a ranger station, and a large parking lot to accommodate the numerous visitors.

Old Faithful erupts approximately 20 times a day, and its eruptions are about 90 percent predictable within a 10-minute variation. The individual eruptions last between 1.5 and 5 minutes and can vary in height from 100 feet to 180 feet. The interval between eruptions is not predictable.

Best Time to Visit: The best time to visit the Old Faithful Geyser is in the spring, summer, or fall.

Pass/Permit/Fees: There is a $35 fee for a 7-day pass to enter Yellowstone National Park and visit the geyser.

Closest City or Town: Cody

Physical Address:
Cody Country Chamber of Commerce Visitor Center
836 Sheridan Avenue
Cody, WY 82414

GPS Coordinates: 44.46068° N, 110.82809° W

Did You Know? Even after a significant earthquake in 1959, Old Faithful remains fairly predictable, erupting just one fewer time per day than before the earthquake.

Old Trail Town

Old Trail Town is a re-created Old West town that was assembled by Bob Edgar with the intention of gathering and preserving historical buildings and associated artifacts that he noticed were rapidly disappearing from the state. In 1967, Edgar began moving historical buildings from their original locations to a site on the west side of Cody. Most of them were completely disassembled, moved to Cody, and reassembled. Currently, there are 26 buildings in Old Trail Town that date between 1876 and 1901. There are also 100 horse-drawn wagons and other vehicles as well as a large collection of authentic Native American artifacts and Wyoming frontier memorabilia.

Best Time to Visit: Old Trail Town is open daily between May 15 and September 30 from 8:00 a.m. to 6:00 p.m.

Pass/Permit/Fees: The fee to visit Old Trail Town is $10 for adults, $9 for seniors over the age of 65, and $5 for kids between the ages of 6 and 12. Children ages 5 and under are free.

Closest City or Town: Cody

Physical Address:
18301 Demaris Drive
Cody, WY 82414

GPS Coordinates: 44.51558° N, 109.10437° W

Did You Know? Old Trail Town was named the "Best Tourist Attraction and Historical Site" by *True West Magazine*.

Sheepeater Cliff

Sheepeater Cliff is an exposed cliff in Yellowstone National Park that is a perfect example of basaltic flow from the basaltic floods in the Yellowstone area approximately 500,000 years ago. The main characteristic of cliffs formed by basaltic flow is the presence of hexagonal columns that are evenly spaced across the cliff. Sheepeater Cliff is made up of a series of vertical columns that, when viewed from the top, are hexagonal in shape. They are all so similar that the formation almost looks man-made. This pattern is the result of extremely slow-cooling lava that once flowed from a volcano. The hexagonal shape is naturally stronger against the thermal stress that's created as the rock cools, which is why it is the most commonly seen shape at Sheepeater Cliff.

Best Time to Visit: The best time to visit Sheepeater Cliff is in the spring, summer, or fall.

Pass/Permit/Fees: There is a $35 fee for a 7-day pass to enter Yellowstone National Park and visit the cliff.

Closest City or Town: Cody

Physical Address:
Cody Country Chamber of Commerce Visitor Center
836 Sheridan Avenue
Cody, WY 82414

GPS Coordinates: 44.93675° N, 110.67677° W

Did You Know? This column rock feature is in several places at Yellowstone, but Sheepeater Cliff is the only place you can walk up to the formation.

Smith Mansion

Built by engineer Francis "Lee" Smith, the Smith Mansion is an eclectic house constructed of wood salvaged from a Rattlesnake Mountain fire. While it looked fairly unremarkable at first, Smith continued to add to the home, constructing extra floors, balconies, and other structures, all from leftover logs. As a result, the mansion looks haphazardly built, with no set pattern or plan. Winding staircases and terraces stick out of the structure at odd angles. The Smith Mansion is currently empty, and at one time, Lee Smith's daughter Sunny Smith Larsen hoped to raise the funds to open the house to the public as a museum. Unfortunately, before that could happen, the building was sold to a tourism and lodging company in 2019; what happens to the mansion from there has yet to be determined. Visitors are unable to go inside the mansion, but it is easily viewable from the road.

Best Time to Visit: The best time to visit the Smith Mansion is in the spring, summer, or fall during the day.

Pass/Permit/Fees: There is no fee to visit the mansion.

Closest City or Town: Cody

Physical Address:
2902 North Fork Highway
Cody, WY 82414

GPS Coordinates: 44.46197° N, 109.49442° W

Did You Know? In 1992, Lee Smith fell to his death while working untethered on an upper balcony of the mansion.

The Buffalo Bill Center of the West

Five museums make up the Buffalo Bill Center of the West. The Draper Natural History Museum focuses on Yellowstone's sensory experiences through wildlife and plant exhibits. The Buffalo Bill Museum features all things Buffalo Bill from his birth to his death. The Plains Indian Museum allows visitors to learn firsthand about the cultures, traditions, and histories of the Plains Indian peoples. The Whitney Western Art Museum features a premier collection of western art, and the Cody Fireworks Museum is home to over 4,000 firearms.

Best Time to Visit: The center is open from May 1 to September 15 from 8:00 a.m. to 6:00 p.m. Hours vary between September 16 and April 30. Check the center's website for details.

Pass/Permit/Fees: The fee to visit the Buffalo Bill Center of the West is $22 for adults, $20 for students, $21 for seniors, and $15 for children between the ages of 6 and 17. Children ages 5 and under are free.

Closest City or Town: Cody

Physical Address:
720 Sheridan Avenue
Cody, WY 82414

GPS Coordinates: 44.52518° N, 109.07318° W

Did You Know? Buffalo Bill Cody was a cowboy famous for founding *Buffalo Bill's Wild West* show in 1882.

The Crow's Nest

Located on the third floor of the Old Faithful Inn in Yellowstone, the Crow's Nest is an indoor treehouse that also features several catwalks. From there, a set of stairs climb to a deck perched on the very top of the roof. The Crow's Nest, which is 76 feet above the ground, was designed by architect Robert Reamer as a physical fulfillment of a childhood dream. When the Crow's Nest was first built, an orchestra would play their instruments from the treehouse portion, providing mood music for the guests on the ground floor. In 1959, an earthquake in Yellowstone damaged both the inn and the Crow's Nest, forcing both to close to the public for a period of time. While the inn eventually reopened to the public, the Crow's Nest never did. Today's guests can see the winding staircase that leads up to the Crow's Nest and view the treehouse high in the rafters.

Best Time to Visit: The Crow's Nest can be viewed at any time of the year.

Pass/Permit/Fees: There is a $35 fee for a 7-day pass to enter Yellowstone National Park and visit the Crow's Nest.

Closest City or Town: Cody

Physical Address:
3200 Old Faithful Inn Road
Yellowstone National Park, WY 82190

GPS Coordinates: 44.46118° N, 110.83666° W

Did You Know? The logs that were used to build the Crow's Nest are still in place today.

The Wreck of the *E.C. Waters*

At the turn of the 20th century, E.C. Waters saw an opportunity to make money from the spectacular landscape and rich resources in Yellowstone National Park. As such, he launched a successful passenger steamship on Yellowstone Lake. The *Zillah* was one of Waters's better ideas. Waters wasn't a pleasant man and got in trouble for his volatile personality. That didn't stop him from buying a second steamship in 1905 that was significantly larger than the *Zillah*. Waters named it the *E.C. Waters* and began taking as many as 500 people on tours of Yellowstone Lake. Waters's relationship with the park continued to decline to the point that he was banned from Yellowstone and wasn't able to retrieve his ship. Eventually, the ship deteriorated and was left to rot.

Best Time to Visit: The best time to visit the wreck of the *E.C. Waters* is in the spring, summer, or fall.

Pass/Permit/Fees: There is a $35 fee for a 7-day pass to enter Yellowstone National Park and view the wreck.

Closest City or Town: Cody

Physical Address:
Cody Country Chamber of Commerce Visitor Center
836 Sheridan Avenue
Cody, WY 82414

GPS Coordinates: 44.51078° N, 110.38193° W

Did You Know? At various times, the destroyed *E.C. Waters* has been used as an overhang for a fish-fry business and a place to stage bar fights.

Tower Fall

Tower Fall is a spectacular waterfall that plunges 132 feet over rock columns in Yellowstone National Park. Photographs and paintings of this waterfall convinced Congress to name Yellowstone the world's first national park. William Henry Jackson first photographed the gorgeous falls in 1871, and when he and artist Thomas Moran returned from their visit to the Yellowstone area, their artwork sparked massive interest in the falls and other natural features. Just a year later in 1872, Yellowstone National Park was created. Until 1986, there was a giant boulder perched right at the edge of the falls where it drops to the pool below, but in June of that year, it fell from its precarious spot over the falls. You can see the boulder in the early photographs and paintings of Tower Fall.

Best Time to Visit: The best time to visit Tower Fall is in the spring, summer, or fall.

Pass/Permit/Fees: There is a $35 fee for a 7-day pass to enter Yellowstone National Park and visit Tower Fall.

Closest City or Town: Cody

Physical Address:
Cody Country Chamber of Commerce Visitor Center
836 Sheridan Avenue
Cody, WY 82414

GPS Coordinates: 44.89402° N, 110.38713° W

Did You Know? Tower Fall takes its name from the towering spires formed from volcanic eruptions that surround Tower Creek.

Upper Geyser Basin

The Upper Geyser Basin in Yellowstone National Park is the most visited destination in the park as it is home to at least 250 hydrothermal geysers. The most famous geyser in the world, Old Faithful, is located here, along with four other major geysers. These five geysers erupt on a more-or-less predictable basis, with park rangers keeping track of their eruptions to help guests plan their visit. Old Faithful is the most predictable of the major geysers in the Upper Geyser Basin. The Morning Glory Pool is located at the northern end of the basin. Be sure to also spend some time on Geyser Hill, which features more than 40 geysers, vents, and pools.

Best Time to Visit: The best time to visit the Upper Geyser Basin is in the spring, summer, or fall.

Pass/Permit/Fees: There is a $35 fee for a 7-day pass to enter Yellowstone National Park and view the basin.

Closest City or Town: Cody

Physical Address:
Cody Country Chamber of Commerce Visitor Center
836 Sheridan Avenue
Cody, WY 82414

GPS Coordinates: 44.46273° N, 110.82939° W

Did You Know? The Upper Geyser Basin is just 2 square miles in size but holds the largest concentration (nearly 25 percent) of all geothermal geysers in the world.

Yellowstone National Park

The 2.2-million-acre Yellowstone National Park offers unparalleled access to rare geothermal features, wildlife in their natural habitats, and geologic marvels that rival any landscape in the nation. In an area larger than Delaware and Rhode Island combined, Yellowstone hosts approximately 4.86 million visitors every year, many of them drawn to famous features such as the Old Faithful geyser, Mammoth Hot Springs, Tower Fall, Morning Glory Pool, the Grand Prismatic Spring, Yellowstone Lake, Mount Washburn, and more. This is not a national park that can be seen in just a day. Plan to spend at least 2–3 days viewing all the major attractions and a few of the smaller hidden gems.

Best Time to Visit: The best time to visit Yellowstone National Park is in the spring, summer, or fall.

Pass/Permit/Fees: There is a $35 fee for a 7-day pass to enter Yellowstone National Park.

Closest City or Town: Cody

Physical Address:
Cody Country Chamber of Commerce Visitor Center
836 Sheridan Avenue
Cody, WY 82414

GPS Coordinates: 44.43103° N, 110.58811° W

Did You Know? Yellowstone National Park is named after the Yellowstone River, which was called *Roche Jaune*, or "Yellow Rock River," by early 18th-century French trappers. It was incorrectly translated to English as "Yellow Stone.

Ayres Natural Bridge

Ayres Natural Bridge, located south of the Oregon Trail, is one of just three natural bridges in the country with water underneath it. It is situated in a public park that is a favorite destination for group events such as birthday parties, family reunions, weddings, and company picnics. Besides the stunning view of the bridge, park amenities include a playground, a sand volleyball court, hiking paths, fishing areas, and horseshoe pits. Ayres Natural Bridge is also a popular place for photographs, as there are numerous challenging angles that provide both professional and amateur photographers with an opportunity to capture the perfect shot. Before the bridge became a tourist attraction, it was considered evil by the Native Americans in the area. This was because a young brave who was hunting in the canyon was struck and killed by lightning. This gave rise to the legend that an evil spirit lived under the bridge.

Best Time to Visit: The Ayres Natural Bridge is only open between April 15 and October 15.

Pass/Permit/Fees: There is no fee to visit.

Closest City or Town: Douglas

Physical Address:
208 Natural Bridge Road
Douglas, WY 82633

GPS Coordinates: 42.73428° N, 105.61149° W

Did You Know? The Ayres Natural Bridge is considered Wyoming's first tourist attraction since travelers along the Oregon Trail would visit the bridge on their way west.

Former World's Largest Jackalope

Wyoming is the land of the mythical jackalope, a cross between a jackrabbit and an antelope that was first conceived in the 1930s when two taxidermists named the Herrick brothers affixed antelope antlers to jackrabbit bodies. They sold well and the trend continued to spread, with jackalopes appearing on wall mounts everywhere throughout the west.

The Former World's Largest Jackalope is 8 feet tall and actually the second incarnation of this creature. The first was built in 1965 and placed in a traffic median but was destroyed by a car in the 1990s. The new one was built and placed in Jackalope Square, where it still remains. Later, in 2007, after the jackalope became Wyoming's official mythical creature, the city purchased an even larger jackalope that is nearly 16 feet tall. It was placed in front of the Douglas Railroad Interpretive Center.

Best Time to Visit: Visit this attraction any time of year.

Pass/Permit/Fees: There is no fee to visit.

Closest City or Town: Douglas

Physical Address:
100 S. 3rd Street
Douglas, WY 82633

GPS Coordinates: 42.75960° N, 105.38412° W

Did You Know? Douglas, home of the Former World's Largest Jackalope, has the goal of building an 80-foot-tall fiberglass Jackalope to restore their previous reputation.

Thunder Basin National Grassland

Located in Medicine Bow-Routt National Forest, the Thunder Basin National Grassland encompasses nearly 2.9 million acres of land that offer an abundance of recreational opportunities. Hiking, hunting, fishing, and sightseeing are just some of the more popular activities for visitors. The land also provides wildlife and livestock with grass for foraging, and it's not uncommon to see foxes, pronghorns, prairie dogs, elk, antelope, coyotes, and even wild turkeys. The black-tailed prairie dog is critical for this environment because it burrows and crops vegetation to create habitats for other species. The grasslands are located between the Black Hills and the Bighorn Mountains, making it one of the most scenic locations in the state. Grasslands are the least protected habitat on the planet, and the Thunder Basin National Grassland seeks to keep this national resource intact despite the number of threats to it.

Best Time to Visit: The best time to visit the Thunder Basin National Grassland is in the spring, summer, or fall.

Pass/Permit/Fees: There is no fee to visit the Thunder Basin National Grasslands.

Closest City or Town: Douglas

Physical Address:
2250 E. Richards Street
Douglas, WY 82633

GPS Coordinates: 43.84817° N, 104.86205° W

Did You Know? There are no developed campgrounds in the grassland, but primitive camping is allowed.

Bitterroot Ranch

The Bitterroot Ranch provides visitors with some of the most diverse horseback-riding adventures in the country. It is bordered by the Shoshone National Forest and provides stunning views of the Absaroka Mountains and the Wind River. Bitterroot Ranch is both a guest and working ranch that was established in 1971 by Bayard Fox and his wife Mel. Most of the horses on the ranch have been born there and are allowed to roam in a large pasture every afternoon. The herd includes mustangs, Appaloosas, Quarter Horses, Percherons, Welsh ponies, and Spanish and CMK Arabians. Along with horseback-riding trips and retreats, visitors can choose to participate in yoga, pack trips, cattle work and roundups, and instructional clinics.

Best Time to Visit: Bitterroot Ranch closes in December and reopens in May.

Pass/Permit/Fees: The fee to visit Bitterroot Ranch depends on the program you choose. They range from $1,700 to $3,450 per person. Contact the ranch directly at 1-800-545-0019 for pricing details.

Closest City or Town: Dubois

Physical Address:
1480 E. Fork Road
Dubois, WY 82513

GPS Coordinates: 43.61701 ° N, 109.39786° W

Did You Know? Founders Bayard and Mel Fox and their children, Hadley and Richard, personally lead horseback rides nearly every day.

Gannett Peak

Gannett Peak is the highest point in Wyoming at 13,804 feet. It is situated in the Wind River Range and is the most isolated mountain in the state. Due to its remoteness, glacier and rock travel, and unpredictable weather patterns, Gannett Peak is considered one of the most difficult state high-point mountains to summit in the nation. Since there is nowhere to camp on the peak, climbers have to be prepared for a 20-hour day to hike to the summit and back, with some of the trip including snow and glaciers. Outside of fishing, camping, and hiking, there are few activities available on Gannett Peak because of its remoteness and ruggedness. Beware of bears, which are common in the Wind River Range, and regardless of the season, be prepared for snow and other adverse weather conditions.

Best Time to Visit: The best time to hike to the summit of Gannett Peak is between April and September.

Pass/Permit/Fees: There is no fee to visit Gannett Peak.

Closest City or Town: Dubois

Physical Address:
Dubois Visitor Center
20 Stainaker Street
Dubois, WY 82513

GPS Coordinates: 43.18727° N, 109.65387° W

Did You Know? Gannett Glacier on Gannett Peak is the largest single glacier in the Rocky Mountains at 896 acres in size.

Bear River State Park

Bear River State Park is a year-round park that provides 300 acres of land for hiking, picnicking, bicycling, wildlife observation, rollerblading, and skiing. There is a herd of bison and elk in the park that is available for public viewing, and 3 miles of foot trails exist within the park limits. There are 1.2 miles of paved paths that feature an arched footbridge over the Bear River and 1.7 miles of packed gravel paths on the west side of the river. These trails double as cross-country ski paths in the winter, and several other trails are groomed specifically for skiing and snowshoeing. Numerous public events are held in the park each year, including the Bear River Rendezvous, which is held the weekend before Labor Day.

Best Time to Visit: Bear River State Park is open year round from 8:00 a.m. to 10:00 p.m. between May 1 and September 30 and from 8:00 a.m. to 8:00 p.m. between October 1 and April 30.

Pass/Permit/Fees: There is no fee to visit the park.

Closest City or Town: Evanston

Physical Address:
601 Bear River Drive
Evanston, WY 82930

GPS Coordinates: 41.26430° N, 110.93581° W

Did You Know? Bear River Park was established in 1991 and named for the river that passes through it. Bear River was named by trappers who would frequently see bears in the area.

Porter's Liquor and Fireworks Outlet

Located just over the border from Utah, Porter's Liquor and Fireworks Outlet provides easy access to two items that are banned in eastern Utah: liquor and fireworks. Situated just off I-80, tourists can easily find the store by following the giant billboard that announces "Liquor and Fireworks." The company originally opened in 1950 when Kilburn Porter and his brother Grant opened a drive-in and gas station called Porter's Cut-O-King. A traveling salesman convinced the family to sell fireworks at the drive-in, and Grant's son Dennis further championed the idea, and a new revenue stream was born. run by the Porter family.

Best Time to Visit: Porter's Liquor and Fireworks Outlet is open Saturday through Thursday from 8:00 a.m. to 10:00 p.m. and Friday from 8:00 a.m. to 11:00 p.m.

Pass/Permit/Fees: There is no fee to visit Porter's Liquor and Fireworks Outlet, but you will need money if you intend to buy either alcohol or fireworks.

Closest City or Town: Evanston

Physical Location:
755 Overthrust Drive
Evanston, WY 82930

GPS Coordinates: 41.25761° N, 110.98949° W

Did You Know? Porter's Liquor and Fireworks Outlet boasts 12,000 square feet of space filled with commercially available fireworks.

Bighorn Medicine Wheel

The Bighorn Medicine Wheel is located in Bighorn National Forest. This national historic landmark commemorates a major Native American sacred site and archaeological property that has been used by various Native American tribes. The 4,080 acres include numerous natural formations and vistas that are associated with ceremonial and cultural activities of these tribes. The Bighorn Medicine Wheel is included, and it's one of the largest stone medicine wheels in North America. The Medicine Wheel is located on the limestone ridge of Medicine Mountain at 9,640 feet above sea level. This set of stones is positioned in a roughly circular shape that's approximately 82 feet in diameter. It surrounds a central stone cairn that is about 12 feet in diameter. There is a hollow oval rock cairn in the center of the pattern from which 28 radial lines extend to another circle on the perimeter of the pattern.

Best Time to Visit: Visit in the spring, summer, or fall.

Pass/Permit/Fees: There is no fee to visit.

Closest City or Town: Greybull

Physical Address:
95 Highway 16/20
Greybull, WY 82434

GPS Coordinates: 44.82637° N, 107.92160° W

Did You Know? The Bighorn Medicine Wheel could be as old as 3,000 years and continues to be a place of ceremony for Native Americans today.

Medicine Mountain

Medicine Mountain is the location of the Bighorn Medicine Wheel, a national historic landmark that is located along a limestone plateau near the crest of the Bighorn Mountains. In addition to the Medicine Wheel, Medicine Mountain has been a major traditional and ceremonial area for numerous Native American Tribes, including the Bannock, Crow, Cheyenne, Arapaho, Blackfeet, Plains Cree, Sioux, Shoshone, Plains Cree, and Kootenai-Salish tribes.

The various rock alignments and cairns that have been discovered on Medicine Mountain are religious in nature and are actually more important to these tribes than the Medicine Wheel. Until it was designated a natural historic landmark, Medicine Mountain was a highly valued hunting, fishing, and camping location. It also offered various economical resources such as lumber, ore, and bighorn sheep to the local population.

Best Time to Visit: The best time to visit Medicine Mountain is in the spring, summer, or fall.

Pass/Permit/Fees: There is no fee to visit.

Closest City or Town: Greybull

Physical Address:
95 Highway 16/20
Greybull, WY 82434

GPS Coordinates: 44.81958° N, 107.90093° W

Did You Know? Native Americans still perform ceremonies on Medicine Mountain.

Museum of Flight and Aerial Firefighting

The Museum of Flight and Aerial Firefighting was created primarily to preserve a component of aviation history, aerial firefighting, that is often not included in other aviation museums. It was founded in 1987 and originally showcased the firefighting fleet of Hawkins & Powers Aviation, Inc. Hawkins & Powers conducted firefighting operations for years out of the South Big Horn County Airport in Greybull.

When two Hawkins & Powers planes crashed during firefighting operations in 2002, their remaining planes were grounded, and eventually, the company was forced to sell its assets at an auction. The museum was threatened, but the U.S. Forest Service and private citizens donated several planes to keep the museum's vision alive.

Best Time to Visit: The Museum of Flight and Aerial Firefighting is open Monday through Saturday between mid-May and October 2 from 9:00 a.m. to 5:00 p.m.

Pass/Permit/Fees: There is no fee to visit.

Closest City or Town: Greybull

Physical Address:
2534 Hiller Lane
Greybull, WY 82426

GPS Coordinates: 44.51060° N, 108.081515° W

Did You Know? According to the Museum of Flight and Aerial Firefighting, planes were being used to fight fires as soon as 16 years after the first airplane took off.

66

Register Cliff

Register Cliff was a major landmark along the Oregon Trail and the first night's camp for travelers west of Fort Laramie. The cliff is 100 feet above the North Platte River, making it an ideal place for travelers to set up camp, put their animals out to pasture, and rest before resuming their journey west the next day. Since travelers had time to spare during the stopover, many of them recorded their names and the dates of their visit on the rock face of the cliff. Visitors today can see inscriptions from the 1840s and 1850s and track pioneers from various eastern states such as Ohio. Register Cliff is such a prominent formation that it probably served as a familiar landmark for travelers well before westward expansion, but most of the inscriptions from that time have disappeared due to erosion. There are three "registers of the desert" along the westward trails in Wyoming, of which Register Cliff is the best-known.

Best Time to Visit: Register Cliff is excellent year-round.

Pass/Permit/Fees: There is no fee to visit.

Closest City or Town: Guernsey

Physical Address:
Guernsey City Visitor Center
90 S. Wyoming Avenue
Guernsey, WY 82214

GPS Coordinates: 42.25048° N, 104.71176° W

Did You Know? The oldest inscription still visible on Register Rock is "1829 This July 14." There is no name associated with this inscription.

Devils Tower National Monument

Devils Tower is a geological rock formation that protrudes out of the ground in the middle of otherwise flat land in the Black Hills area of Wyoming. It was the first national monument in the United States. The Northern Plains Indians and indigenous people consider the formation to be sacred. Many of the oral stories include young Native American tribe members running from wild animals and jumping on a rock to escape. As the animals climbed toward the children, they prayed for the rock to save them. The rock began to grow out from the ground and continued until it was so high that the animals could not reach the children. Not only is the tower sacred, but it's also one of the most famous rock-climbing destinations in the world.

Best Time to Visit: The best time to visit Devils Tower National Monument is between May and October. The best time to climb is May through June.

Pass/Permit/Fees: The fee to visit Devils Tower National Monument is $20 per vehicle or $10 per person. The pass is valid for 7 days.

Closest City or Town: Hulett

Physical Address:
340 WY-110
Devils Tower, WY 82714

GPS Coordinates: 44.59026° N, 104.71464° W

Did You Know? Devils Tower was featured prominently in the blockbuster movie *Close Encounters of the Third Kind.*

Table Mountain Vineyards and Winery

Table Mountain Vineyards and Winery is one of the largest vineyards in Wyoming. There are more than 10,000 grape vines and a full-scale winery on 10 acres of what originally was the Zimmerer family farm. Over the years, the family has grown everything from sugar beets and beans to alfalfa and corn. It was even a feed lot at one point. In 2001, a member of the Zimmerer family, Patrick, convinced the rest of the family to plant a 300-vine vineyard on a small part of their farm. Once they discovered the vines could survive Wyoming's challenging climate, the Zimmerers decided to pivot to full-time winemaking using only grape varieties that can withstand the harsh climate.

Best Time to Visit: Currently, tastings at Table Mountain Vineyards and Winery are only available by appointment. Call 307-459-0233 to check availability.

Pass/Permit/Fees: There is no fee to visit Table Mountain Vineyards and Winery, but be sure to bring money for wine tastings.

Closest City or Town: Huntley

Physical Address:
5933 Road 48
Huntley, WY 82218

GPS Coordinates: 41.89936° N, 104.08541° W

Did You Know? Table Mountain Vineyards and Winery is committed to producing 100 percent of its wine from grapes, raspberries, honey, and other agricultural products grown in Wyoming.

Antelope Flats

Located in the Grand Teton National Park, the 640-acre Antelope Flats is a must-see destination that was established to preserve wildlife habitats and provide migration routes for various species. Visitors to Antelope Flats will also get a glimpse of the Old West since there are several old homesteads on the land that offer breathtaking mountain views. Antelope Flats Road winds through sagebrush-filled plains and features several historic sites like Mormon Row, the Gros Ventre Mountains, and the Blacktail Butte area. You'll experience clear views of the Jackson Hole valley and a stunning panorama of the Tetons' Cathedral Group, which include the Mount Owen, Grand, and Teewinot peaks at the center of the mountain range.

Best Time to Visit: The best time to visit Antelope Flats is between May and September when wildlife is abundant.

Pass/Permit/Fees: There is a $35 fee for a 7-day pass to enter Grand Teton National Park and visit the flats.

Closest City or Town: Jackson

Physical Address:
103 Headquarters Loop
Moose, WY 83012

GPS Coordinates: 43.70571° N, 110.64775° W

Did You Know? In 2016, the U.S. Department of the Interior purchased Antelope Flats from the Wyoming State Educational Trust to protect the wildlife in the area.

A-OK Corral

The A-OK Corral offers cowboy experiences for the entire family. From horseback rides through the Gros Ventre Wilderness to rafting along the Snake River, you'll get to enjoy the Wyoming wilderness and all it has to offer. Located near Jackson Hole, the A-OK Corral is designed for visitors who want to rough it without *really* roughing it. You can stay in a comfortable hotel in the city and have an adventurous day out on the range at the A-OK Corral. Shorter horseback rides range from the 1-hour Snake River Ride to longer excursions like the Full-Day Horse Creek Wilderness Ride. You can also add fishing to the adventure with the All-Day Fishing Ride, which includes lunch and fishing gear.

Best Time to Visit: The A-OK Corral is only open from late spring through the fall, with spring seeing fewer crowds.

Pass/Permit/Fees: Horseback rides at the A-OK Corral start at $65 per person for the 1-hour ride. The rafting and fishing packages start at $695 per person.

Closest City or Town: Jackson

Physical Address:
9600 S. U.S. Highway 89
Jackson, Wyoming 83001

GPS Coordinates: 43.34266° N, 110.72130° W

Did You Know? The name for A-OK Corral is inspired by the famous shootout between Virgil Earp and lawmen that took place in Tombstone, Arizona in 1881.

Bar T 5

The Bar T 5 is Jackson Hole's original chuckwagon experience that provides visitors with a true western adventure. This includes a horse-drawn covered-wagon ride through the Cache Creek Canyon; a savory authentic chuckwagon all-you-can-eat dinner; and live, hand-clapping entertainment from the Bar T 5 Band. During dinner, you'll meet Buckskin, a friendly mountain man who will entertain you as he chases off the "pesky outlaws" trying to steal your dessert. The Bar T 5 Band sings traditional western music, but don't let your guard down. The show is interactive, which means you could be pulled up on stage at any moment. The adventure ends with a second covered-wagon ride back through the canyon as the sun sets, providing a spectacular, scenic finale.

Best Time to Visit: Bar T 5 only operates between mid-May and the end of September and requires reservations.

Pass/Permit/Fees: The fee to participate in the Bar T 5 chuckwagon experience is $60 for adults and $45 for children between the ages of 5 and 12.

Closest City or Town: Jackson

Physical Address:
812 Cache Creek Drive
Jackson, WY 83001

GPS Coordinates: 43.47268° N, 110.74470° W

Did You Know? Bar T 5 is a family operation with roots going back to 1856 when Elijah Nicholas Wilson ran away from home and settled in the Jackson area.

Bridger-Teton National Forest

More than 3.4 million acres are available for public recreation within the Bridger-Teton National Forest. It features abundant opportunities for outdoor activities like camping, fishing, hiking, horseback riding, hunting, bicycling, scenic driving, boating, swimming, wildlife observation, picnicking, off-roading, downhill skiing, snowboarding, cross-country skiing, snowshoeing, and even mushing. There are over 3,000 miles of roads and trails throughout the forest, ensuring there is something for everyone. Outside of Alaska, the Bridger-Teton National Forest is the third largest in the United States and extends from Yellowstone National Park to the southern end of the Wind River Range in the Rocky Mountains. Gannett Peak is the tallest mountain in the forest, towering 13,804 feet above sea level.

Best Time to Visit: The best time to visit is between mid-May and late September for comfortable weather.

Pass/Permit/Fees: There is no fee to visit.

Closest City or Town: Jackson

Physical Address:
Craig Thomas Discovery & Visitor Center
100 Discovery Way
Moose, WY 83012

GPS Coordinates: 43.92602° N, 110.24268° W

Did You Know? Within the Bridger-Teton National Forest, visitors can see the Gros Ventre Landslide, one of the largest on the planet.

Cascade Canyon Trail

The Cascade Canyon Trail in Grand Teton National Park can be as short as 3.4 miles or as long as 9.3 miles round trip. It also features a shuttle-boat ride across Jenny Lake to reach the Cascade Canyon trailhead, which reduces the hiking distance by 4 miles round trip. However, it does require a fee.

If you decide not to take the shuttle boat, the hike involves a 2-mile walk around the lake. The shuttle runs every 10–15 minutes and costs $18 per adult for a round-trip ticket. You may also decide to hike to the Hidden Falls and take a one-way boat ride back to the east side of Jenny Lake for $10. You can extend your hike to Inspiration Point by crossing a wooden bridge and climbing a series of challenging switchbacks up a granite knoll.

Best Time to Visit: The best time to visit Cascade Canyon Trail is in late spring, early summer, or after a heavy rain.

Pass/Permit/Fees: There is a $35 fee for a 7-day pass to enter Grand Teton National Park and visit the trail.

Closest City or Town: Jackson

Physical Address:
103 Headquarters Loop
Moose, WY 83012

GPS Coordinates: 43.76373° N, 110.78141° W

Did You Know? Hidden Falls is a prominent waterfall that features an impressive 200-foot drop down several tiers of rock.

Jackson

Jackson is situated on the southern end of the valley known as Jackson Hole. Originally, the area where the town is located was inhabited by numerous Native American and indigenous tribes, including Bannock, Blackfoot, Crow, Gros Ventre, and Shoshone, among others. During the Lewis and Clark expedition's return journey in 1807 and 1808, John Colter visited the Jackson Hole area, and it subsequently became a popular location for trappers and mountain men.

Jackson was named in 1894 and established as a town in 1914. It remains the only incorporated municipality in Teton County. There are three world-class ski resorts in Jackson Hole, including Snow King Resort, which is located in the town of Jackson itself.

Best Time to Visit: Jackson is a great place to visit year round but is especially popular in the winter for skiing.

Pass/Permit/Fees: There is no fee to visit Jackson.

Closest City or Town: Jackson

Physical Address:
Jackson Hole & Greater Yellowstone Visitor Center
532 N. Cache Street
Jackson, WY 83001

GPS Coordinates: 43.49069° N, 110.75191° W

Did You Know? Jackson is named for David Edward Jackson, an American pioneer, fur trader, trapper, and explorer who spent a winter in the area.

Jackson Hole Children's Museum

The Jackson Hole Children's Museum opened in 2011. It was the dream of KJ and Craig Morris, who wanted to provide an environment for children where they could play, explore, discover, innovate, create, and collaborate. Along with the support of more than 100 local donors, their vision became reality, establishing a museum where children instinctively know what to do. Interactive exhibits at the museum include *The Climber*, *The Magnet Wall*, *Wild Wind Machine*, *Mountain Market*, *Dig Pit*, *Light Box*, and others. There is also the *Tot Spot*, which is a special play area designed just for children under the age of 3. The Outdoor Classroom is a 15-person space designed as a place where kids can make a "big, spectacular mess!"

Best Time to Visit: The museum is open Monday through Friday from 9:00 a.m. to 4:00 p.m. and Saturday from 12:00 p.m. to 4:30 p.m. Members have an additional time on Saturdays between 9:00 a.m. and 11:00 a.m.

Pass/Permit/Fees: The fee to visit the Jackson Hole Children's Museum is $10 per person for visitors ages 2 and older. Children under the age of 2 are free.

Closest City or Town: Jackson

Physical Address:
155 N. Jean Street
Jackson, WY 83001

GPS Coordinates: 43.48212° N, 110.75734° W

Did You Know? The Jackson Hole Children's Museum is also known as The Clubhouse.

Jackson Hole Mountain Resort

Jackson Hole Mountain Resort is the most famous ski resort in Wyoming. It is known for its challenging terrain on both Rendezvous and Après Vous mountains. In fact, half of the terrain is rated expert, 40 percent is rated intermediate, and just 10 percent is rated beginner. Rendezvous Mountain is where skiers and snowboarders will find more advanced terrain, while the intermediate runs are primarily located on the south-facing Après Vous Mountains. The resort offers 4,000 vertical feet for skiing and snowboarding, which is one of the steepest ski areas in the United States. Skiers and snowboarders who are equipped with avalanche safety gear can also explore an even larger part of the ski resort out of bounds. Jackson Hole Mountain Resort first opened to the public in 1965, and the ariel tram followed in 1966.

Best Time to Visit: The best time to visit Jackson Hole Mountain Resort is in the winter.

Pass/Permit/Fees: The fee to visit varies based on the day. Ski-lift ticket prices range from $150 to $167 per person.

Closest City or Town: Jackson

Physical Address:
3395 Cody Lane
Teton Village, WY 83025

GPS Coordinates: 43.58765° N, 110.82768° W

Did You Know? Prior to becoming a ski resort, Jackson Hole Mountain Resort was the Crystal Springs Girl Scout Ranch.

Jackson Lake

Located in Grand Teton National Park, Jackson Lake is a natural lake that was enlarged when the Jackson Lake Dam was constructed in 1911. It grew again in 1916 and 1989 when the dam was expanded and rebuilt. This 25,540-acre lake is one of the biggest high-altitude lakes in the U.S. with an elevation of 6,772 feet above sea level. While the water is generally too cold for prolonged swimming, it is a popular place for kayaking, boating, and fishing. You can expect to find cutthroat trout, brook trout, brown trout, mountain whitefish, and pike in the deep waters of Jackson Lake. Along the eastern shore, you'll find several marinas and lodges available for supplies, rentals, and accommodations. On the western shore, though, you'll only find hiking trails and a small number of primitive campgrounds.

Best Time to Visit: The best time to visit Jackson Lake for fishing is between June and September.

Pass/Permit/Fees: There is a $35 fee for a 7-day pass to enter Grand Teton National Park and visit Jackson Lake.

Closest City or Town: Jackson

Physical Address:
Jackson Hole & Greater Yellowstone Visitor Center
532 N. Cache Street
Jackson, WY 83001

GPS Coordinates: 43.90258° N, 110.67432° W

Did You Know? Jackson Lake has more than 15 islands, the largest of which is Elk Island.

Laurance S. Rockefeller Preserve

Located in Grand Teton National Park, the Laurance S. Rockefeller Preserve offers a unique opportunity to commune with nature in an environment specifically designed for solitude and reflection. There are several hiking trails that begin in the preserve, including an easy hike to Phelps Lake or a more challenging trail into Granite Canyon or Death Canyon. The Laurance S. Rockefeller Preserve Center is a great way for visitors to discover more about Mr. Rockefeller's dream of land conservation and the preserve that resulted. It offers several interactive exhibits that showcase the sensory qualities of the plants and wildlife in the preserve. You'll also learn about the center's innovative design that makes it a fantastic example of energy conservation and environmental protection.

Best Time to Visit: The best time to visit the Laurance S. Rockefeller Preserve is in the spring, summer, or fall.

Pass/Permit/Fees: There is a $35 fee for a 7-day pass to enter Grand Teton National Park and visit the preserve.

Closest City or Town: Jackson

Physical Address:
Jackson Hole & Greater Yellowstone Visitor Center
532 N. Cache Street
Jackson, WY 83001

GPS Coordinates: 42.62703° N, 110.77341° W

Did You Know? The number of visitors to the Laurance S. Rockefeller Preserve is limited to 300 per day to fulfill Rockefeller's vision of a peaceful, uncrowded natural site.

National Elk Refuge

The National Elk Refuge is a vitally important winter range for several species, including elk, wolves, bison, bighorn sheep, bald eagles, trumpeter swans, and cutthroat trout. The refuge is in a valley that's surrounded by the Teton and Gros Ventre mountain ranges, and it's made up of 24,700 acres of forests, grasslands, and wetlands that provide habitats for a wide range of animals and plants. Visitors will come across antlers that have been shed from elk, and it is important to note that it is "illegal to take, collect, retrieve, posses, or transport any natural product, including shed antlers, from the refuge at any time of the year." Hunting on the refuge is allowed between October 12 and December 12, and fishing on the Gros Ventre River and the Upper Flat Creek is available between April 1 and November 30 each year.

Best Time to Visit: The best time to visit the refuge to see elk is between mid-December and early April.

Pass/Permit/Fees: There is no fee to visit the National Elk Refuge. There may be a fee for activities.

Closest City or Town: Jackson

Physical Address:
675 E. Broadway Avenue
Jackson, WY 83001

GPS Coordinates: 43.47978° N, 110.74328° W

Did You Know? Since 1965, the National Elk Refuge has offered sleigh rides through the area between December and April to view hundreds of elk.

National Museum of Wildlife Art

More than 550 artists and over 5,000 pieces of animal art await visitors at the National Museum of Wildlife Art. As the only museum in the nation dedicated solely to wildlife art, this museum provides education, inspiration, and appreciation of man's relationship with animals and nature through art.

Take a walk on the museum's outdoor trail to view life-size animal sculptures of bison, elk, bears, and more, or check out the indoor galleries and exhibits. The museum was founded in 1987 and features permanent art from artists such as Andy Warhol, Georgia O'Keeffe, Carl Rungius, and more.

Best Time to Visit: The museum is open Tuesday through Sunday from 10:00 a.m. to 5:00 p.m.

Pass/Permit/Fees: The fee to visit the National Museum of Wildlife Art is $17 for adults, $8 for the first child between the ages of 5 and 18, $4 for each subsequent child, and $15 for seniors. Children ages 4 and under are free.

Closest City or Town: Jackson

Physical Address:
2820 Rungius Road
Jackson, WY 83001

GPS Coordinates: 43.51971° N, 110.74874° W

Did You Know? The National Museum of Wildlife Art is perfectly situated overlooking the National Elk Refuge.

Oxbow Bend

A popular place for photographers, this overlook along highways 89 and 191 between Moran Junction and Jackson Lake Junction provides a view of the crescent-shaped section of Snake River. The area is home to a wide range of birds and animals, including moose, bear, muskrats, otters, pelicans, and great blue herons. *Oxbow* is the term for this crescent-shaped bend in the river, which is how this overlook got its name.

Photographers tend to visit Oxbow Bend at sunrise or sunset, hoping to capture the perfect image of the river and the Teton Mountain Range. The iconic image of Mount Moran reflected in Snake River was taken from Oxbow Bend and is probably the most recognized photograph of Grand Teton National Park in existence.

Best Time to Visit: The best time to visit Oxbow Bend is in the fall around sunrise or sunset.

Pass/Permit/Fees: There is a $35 fee for a 7-day pass to enter Grand Teton National Park and visit Oxbow Bend.

Closest City or Town: Jackson

Physical Address:
103 Headquarters Loop
Moose, WY 83012

GPS Coordinates: 43.86581° N, 110.54899° W

Did You Know? In the early mornings, visitors to Oxbow Bend will hear the elk bugling.

Parting of the Waters

This one-of-a-kind hydrologic feature is located at Two Ocean Pass on the Continental Divide in the Teton Wilderness section of the Bridger-Teton National Forest. The Parting of the Waters is a phenomenon where the river splits, with the headwaters of Pacific Creek flowing west to the Pacific Ocean and the headwaters of the Atlantic Creek flowing east to the Atlantic Ocean. The waters are divided more or less equally between the two creeks, and it is visually obvious that the river is flowing in two directions. The site is a designated National Natural Landmark, having received that distinction in 1965. Its official name is the Two Ocean Pass National Natural Landmark, but it has been commonly called the Parting of the Waters by locals for decades. From the Parting of the Waters, the water will travel either 3,488 miles to the Atlantic Ocean or 1,353 miles to the Pacific Ocean.

Best Time to Visit: The best time to visit the Parting of the Waters is in the spring, summer, or fall.

Pass/Permit/Fees: There is no fee to visit.

Closest City or Town: Jackson

Physical Address:
Jackson Hole & Greater Yellowstone Visitor Center
532 N. Cache Street
Jackson, WY 83001

GPS Coordinates: 44.04438° N, 110.16673° W

Did You Know? By way of the Parting of the Waters, a fish could feasibly swim from ocean to ocean.

Phelps Lake

Located in Grand Teton National Park, Phelps Lake is a natural body of water located at the entrance to Death Canyon. This 750-acre lake features the Jumping Rock, a point that is situated on the north side that has provided thousands of visitors with a natural diving board. The drop from the rock to the water is between 25 and 30 feet, but the deep water makes it a safe place from which to dive and jump. Phelps Lake is sourced by a glacier, and since the water is cold all year, Jumping Rock is most popular in the summer months. There is also a popular 1.8-mile hiking trail that will take you to the Phelps Lake overlook at 7,800 feet above sea level and back.

Best Time to Visit: The best time to visit Phelps Lake is during the summer, especially if you intend to take a leap off Jumping Rock.

Pass/Permit/Fees: There is no fee to visit Phelps Lake if you use the Death Canyon Trailhead.

Closest City or Town: Jackson

Physical Address:
Jackson Hole & Greater Yellowstone Visitor Center
532 N. Cache Street
Jackson, WY 83001

GPS Coordinates: 43.64650° N, 110.79610° W

Did You Know? Phelps Lake is named for prospector and hunter George Phelps, the first white man to see the lake and one of the prospectors that members of the 1872 Hayden Expedition camped with on July 24 of that year.

Schwabacher Landing

Schwabacher Landing is a spot in Grand Teton National Park along the Snake River where the terrain levels. It is a popular launch site for fishermen and river rafters, and it provides one of the most stunning views in the country. As such, it is a favorite photo opportunity in the park, offering a clear reflection of the Teton Mountains in the calm waters of the Snake River. Visitors may also see wildlife such as deer, antelope, and coyotes in the area when it's not crowded, and along the banks of the Snake River, you can spot sign of beavers, if not the beavers themselves. Beavers in the area constantly work on dams along the river and are most active at dusk and dawn. At times when the water is low, boats may not be able to launch here, which has been happening more often due to drought conditions.

Best Time to Visit: Visit in the summer or fall since the trail can be unpassable at other times due to snow and rain.

Pass/Permit/Fees: There is a $35 fee for a 7-day pass to enter Grand Teton National Park and visit the landing.

Closest City or Town: Jackson

Physical Address:
103 Headquarters Loop
Moose, WY 83012

GPS Coordinates: 43.71170° N, 110.67039° W

Did You Know? Schwabacher Landing is named for ranch owner Albert Schwabacher, who once lived along the east shore of the Snake River in the area.

Taggart Lake

Taggart Lake is a natural lake located in Grand Teton National Park at the terminal end of Avalanche Canyon. There are several popular hiking trails nearby, including a 3-mile round-trip hike that starts at the Taggart Lake Trailhead in the parking area. The lake is fairly small at just 110 acres, but it's considered pristine and untouched by water or air pollution.

The area surrounding Taggart Lake is treeless due to a large wildfire in 1985, which puts the Tetons in full view. The lake's water is cold year round given that it's high in the mountains, but it's an excellent place to fish. Fishermen consider Taggart Lake one of the most challenging fishing spots in Wyoming, but the fabulous scenery makes up for the stubborn fish.

Best Time to Visit: The best time to visit is in the summer.

Pass/Permit/Fees: There is a $35 fee for a 7-day pass to enter Grand Teton National Park and visit the lake.

Closest City or Town: Jackson

Physical Address:
Jackson Hole & Greater Yellowstone Visitor Center
532 N. Cache Street
Jackson, WY 83001

GPS Coordinates: 43.70493° N, 110.75546° W

Did You Know? Taggart Lake takes its name from William Rush Taggart, an assistant surveyor to Frank Bradley during the Hayden expedition of 1872.

T.A. Moulton Barn

The T.A. Moulton Barn is all that is left of the Thomas Alma Moulton homestead in the Mormon Row Historic District. The barn was built by Moulton and his sons at some point between 1912 and 1945. They spent 30 years building the barn, which is why it is still standing today.

Mormon Row was established in the late 1800s when Mormon settlers from Iowa formed a small community near the Teton Mountains. Both amateur and professional photographers flock to the location to take pictures of the scenic barn with the Teton Mountains in the background. Visitors should be sure they're actually capturing and image of the T.A. Moulton Barn and not the nearby barn of his brother John Moulton.

Best Time to Visit: The best time to visit the T.A. Moulton Barn is in late summer or early fall.

Pass/Permit/Fees: There is a $35 fee for a 7-day pass to enter Grand Teton National Park and visit the barn.

Closest City or Town: Jackson

Physical Address:
Jackson Hole & Greater Yellowstone Visitor Center
532 N. Cache Street
Jackson, WY 83001

GPS Coordinates: 43.66090° N, 110.66494° W

Did You Know? The T.A. Moulton Barn was the inspiration for the fictional "most photographed barn in America" in the book *White Noise* by Don DeLillo.

Jeffrey City Ghost Town

What began as a homestead and waystation for weary travelers passing through Wyoming in 1931, Jeffrey City was the center of the uranium-mining industry from the mid-1950s until the mine closed in 1982. At its peak in 1979, there were 4,500 residents in Jeffrey City, supported by a medical clinic, churches, hotels, schools, and numerous shops along Main Street. Once the mine closed, residents struggled to find other work, and when radiation was discovered in their homes, they began fleeing the area in droves. By 1985, only 5 percent of Jeffrey City's once-booming population remained, and by 2010, just 58 people lived in the general vicinity of the town. Today, the structures, roads, streetlights, and park remain, but all are boarded up and abandoned.

Best Time to Visit: The best time to visit Jeffrey City Ghost Town is in the spring, summer, or fall.

Pass/Permit/Fees: There is no fee to visit.

Closest City or Town: Jeffrey City

Physical Address:
Split Rock Gas Station
2297 WY-789
Jeffrey City, WY 82310

GPS Coordinates: 42.50494° N, 107.82582° W

Did You Know? The uranium mine in Jeffery City has been reopened with a 15-year goal of extracting at least 15 million pounds of uranium from the ground.

Hole-in-the-Wall Hideout

Between the 1860s and 1910, the Hole-in-the-Wall Hideout was a notorious stop along the outlaw trail. It was one of the most famous hideouts for many outlaws, including Butch Cassidy's Wild Bunch, the Roberts Brothers, Jack Ketchum, Jesse James, and the Logan Brothers. The actual hideout is in a remote, secluded location that's pretty hard to reach and requires a steep climb over loose rock.

The panoramic views from the hiding spot allowed the outlaws to quickly see anyone approaching the area, and the narrowness of the valley allowed them to easily defend their location. Additionally, the hideout was at least a day's journey on horseback from any city or town, which made it even more attractive to outlaws.

Best Time to Visit: The best time to visit Hole-in-the-Wall Hideout is in the spring, summer, or fall.

Pass/Permit/Fees: There is no fee to visit the hideout.

Closest City or Town: Kaycee

Physical Address:
Kaycee Chamber of Commerce
100 Park Avenue
Kaycee, WY 82639

GPS Coordinates: 43.54871° N, 106.81151° W

Did You Know? Hole-in-the-Wall Hideout was one of three main hideouts used by outlaws in the 1800s.

Fossil Butte National Monument

On the flat-topped mountains of southwestern Wyoming's sagebrush desert, visitors will find some of the world's best-preserved fossils of plants, insects, fish, birds, reptiles, and mammals. The fine-grained lake sediments and the cold-water conditions combined to provide the ideal environment for the preservation of articulated skeletons. Such complete fossils are rare, and scientists are able to extract valuable data from these specimens that isn't available anywhere else.

The monument has several interpretive trails available for hiking, and a scenic drive is available as well. Note that the fossils are not visible from these trails, but the visitor center has more than 300 on display.

Best Time to Visit: The best time to visit Fossil Butte National Monument is in the spring, summer, or fall.

Pass/Permit/Fees: There is no fee to visit the monument.

Closest City or Town: Kemmerer

Physical Address:
864 Chicken Creek Road
Kemmerer, WY 83101

GPS Coordinates: 41.85653° N, 110.76245° W

Did You Know? Just 1 percent of Fossil Lake is protected by the National Park Service at Fossil Butte National Monument. Many more fossils are waiting to be discovered and protected as paleontological activities continue to expand.

Sinks Canyon State Park

Named for an interesting geological formation in which the Popo Agie River disappears underground near the mouth of the canyon, Sinks Canyon is a rugged area located at the base of the Wind River Mountains. The river eventually reappears about a quarter mile down the canyon in a calm pool stocked with large rainbow trout. There are several ecosystems represented in the canyon, including sagebrush, conifer forest, aspen meadows, and alpine. As a result, the diversity of birds and wildlife is incredible. Visitors will also be amazed at the number of wildflowers and other plants in the area and the special geology that makes this canyon unique. Popular recreational activities in the canyon include camping, fishing, photography, nature studies, hiking, rock climbing, and mountain biking, among others.

Best Time to Visit: The best time to visit is in the summer.

Pass/Permit/Fees: There is no fee to visit Sinks Canyon State Park unless you intend to camp overnight. Rates for camping vary. See the park's website for details.

Closest City or Town: Lander

Physical Address:
3079 Sinks Canyon Road
Lander, WY 82520

GPS Coordinates: 42.74701° N, 108.81330° W

Did You Know? Archaeologists in Sinks Canyon State Park have discovered hearths and tools that date as far back as the most recent ice age 25,000 years ago.

Fort Laramie

Fort Laramie was initially established as a private fur-trading post, but it became one of the most famous military posts on the northern plains between its founding year of 1834 and its abandonment in 1890. Originally known as Fort William, the structure was small but held the monopoly on the buffalo trade until Fort Platte was built just a mile away. Eventually, Fort William was replaced with the bigger Fort John in an effort to stay competitive in the buffalo trade. In 1849, the U.S. Army purchased Fort John to establish a military presence along the most traveled trails. At this time, the fort was officially renamed Fort Laramie for its location at the confluence of the Laramie and North Platte rivers. Soon, Fort Laramie grew into the main military outpost on the northern plains.

Best Time to Visit: The best time to visit Fort Laramie is in the spring, summer, or fall.

Pass/Permit/Fees: There is no fee to visit Fort Laramie.

Closest City or Town: Laramie

Physical Address:
965 Grey Rocks Road
Fort Laramie, WY 82212

GPS Coordinates: 42.20349° N, 104.55705° W

Did You Know? Several treaty negotiations between the U.S. and the Northern Plains Indian Nations were held at Fort Laramie, including the Horse Creek Treaty of 1851 and the Treaty of 1868 with the Sioux tribe, which is controversial to this day.

Lincoln Highway Monument

This bust of Abraham Lincoln perches upon a 30-foot-tall granite pedestal located at the Summit Rest Area on I-80 just east of Laramie. Known as the Lincoln Highway Monument, artist Robert Russin originally installed the sculpture on nearby Sherman Hill, which overlooked U.S. Highway 30, also known as the Lincoln Highway. Once I-80 was built in 1969, though, the sculpture was moved to the rest area to become the centerpiece of the visitor center located there. The bronze bust was actually built in Mexico City because Russin felt that the extreme temperature changes in Wyoming would not be conducive to creating the artwork. Over an 11-month period, Russin created the 4,500-pound bust in 30 separate pieces, then shipped them in 1958 to Laramie, first by railroad to Denver, CO, then by truck to Wyoming.

Best Time to Visit: The monument is excellent to visit year round.

Pass/Permit/Fees: There is no fee to visit.

Closest City or Town: Laramie

Physical Address:
Laramie Area Visitor Center
800 S. 3rd Street
Laramie, WY 82070

GPS Coordinates: 41.23716° N, 105.43625° W

Did You Know? Approximately 200,000 travelers visit the Summit Rest Area and view the Lincoln Highway Monument each year.

University of Wyoming Geological Museum

The University of Wyoming Geological Museum is dedicated to preserving and displaying Wyoming's past environments. Included in its exhibits is a 75-foot Apatosaurs skeleton and "Big Al," the most complete Allosaurus fossil found so far. A giant copper-plated *Tyrannosaurus rex* statue stands outside the museum. It was constructed by Samuel H. "Doc" Knight. Other exhibits in the museum include a *Diatryma gigantea* skeleton, a *Stegosaurus* skeleton, a *Triceratops* skull, and a *Tyrannosaurus rex* skull, among other fascinating displays. As the museum is part of the University of Wyoming, it functions both as a way to educate the public on Wyoming's prehistoric past and a facility for ongoing scientific research.

Best Time to Visit: The museum is open Monday through Saturday from 10:00 a.m. to 4:00 p.m.

Pass/Permit/Fees: There is no fee to visit the museum.

Closest City or Town: Laramie

Physical Address:
200 N. 9th Street
Laramie, WY 82070

GPS Coordinates: 41.31428° N, 105.58381° W

Did You Know? The University of Wyoming Geological Museum houses over 50,000 catalogued rock, mineral, and fossil specimens.

Vedauwoo

Located in the Medicine Bow-Routt National Forest, Vedauwoo features towering ancient Sherman-granite rock formations consisting of white quartz, pink feldspar, horneblende, and other minerals like mica. The rock formations are approximately 1.4 billion years old and are among the oldest outcrops in Wyoming. The views from the top of these rocks are breathtaking, but the journey up is what really draws people to the area. Vedauwoo is one of the top rock-climbing destinations in the state with a difficulty range of 5.0 to 5.14. If you aren't into rock climbing, there are plenty of smooth trails for hiking, mountain biking, or horseback riding. These trails also vary in difficulty. Fishing, snowshoeing, wildlife viewing, and cross-country skiing are other activities that are popular within this recreation area.

Best Time to Visit: There are activities in Vedauwoo for any time of the year, but for rock climbing, visit in the spring or fall.

Pass/Permit/Fees: There is a $5 day-use fee to visit.

Closest City or Town: Laramie

Physical Address:
Laramie Area Visitor Center
800 S. 3rd Street
Laramie, WY 82070

GPS Coordinates: 41.15461° N, 105.37449° W

Did You Know? *Vedauwoo* is a Native American word (possibly Arapaho) meaning "land of the earthborn spirits."

Woods Landing Resort

Woods Landing Resort offers various accommodation options just off the highway near the Wyoming-Colorado border. Stay in a cabin with all the comforts of home or a larger 8-person private guest house. You can also park your motorhome or camper at one of the convenient RV sites, all of which have water and electricity hookups and access to a separate sewer dump. Whether you're just looking for a comfortable place to lay your head for a night before you hit the road again or you want somewhere to stay that offers access to Medicine Bow National Forest, the Snowy Range Ski Area, or the Laramie River, Woods Landing Resort is a convenient choice. Don't forget to visit the rustic Woods Landing Bar and Café while you're there. This eclectic combination is housed in a log structure listed on the National Register of Historic Places.

Best Time to Visit: The best time to visit Woods Landing Resort is in the spring, summer, or fall.

Pass/Permit/Fees: The fee to visit Woods Landing Resort depends on accommodation and date selection. See the website for pricing details and availability.

Closest City or Town: Laramie

Physical Address:
9 WY-10
Woods Landing-Jelm, WY 82063

GPS Coordinates: 41.11055° N, 106.01255° W

Did You Know? Woods Landing Resort was originally a saloon built in 1883 by Colonel Samuel Woods.

Bridger Valley Historic Byway

The Bridger Valley Historic Byway has seen thousands of visitors throughout the years as the crossroads for the Oregon Trail, the Mormon Trail, the Transcontinental Railroad, the Lincoln Highway, and the Pony Express Route. The byway is a 20-mile loop that takes travelers past some of the state's most important historical sites.

While Fort Bridger, the point of confluence, was once the hub of travel for people traversing the nation, it became obsolete when I-80 was built in 1956. Today, you can access the byway by exiting I-80 at Exit 34 and rejoining I-80 at Exit 48. While on the route, travelers will pass through the towns of Robertson, Millburne, Urie, Mountain View, Lyman, and, of course, Fort Bridger. You should allow at least 2 hours to visit all the historical sites.

Best Time to Visit: The best time to drive the Bridger Valley Historic Byway is in the spring, summer, or fall.

Pass/Permit/Fees: There is no fee to drive the byway.

Closest City or Town: Little America

Physical Address:
37000 I-80BL
Fort Bridger, WY 82933

GPS Coordinates: 41.31850° N, 110.38937° W

Did You Know? Bridger Valley is named for Jim Bridger, an American mountain man and trapper who built a trading post in the area in 1843, just as the Oregon Trail began to gain popularity as a route west.

Granger Stage Station

The Granger Stage Station was built along the Overland Trail in the mid-1800s. Eventually, many trails passed through Granger, including the Mormon Trail, the Pony Express Trail, the Oregon Trail, the California Trail, and the Cherokee Trail. Originally called the Ham's Fork and then South Bend Station when a stone structure was built on the site in 1865, the Granger Street Station got its current name when Union Pacific Railroad construction workers began calling the site *Granger* in 1868. It was designated as a State Historic Site that same year and listed on the National Register of Historic Places in 1970. There are two interpretive signs, the original stage structure, and a monument to the trails at the site.

Best Time to Visit: The best time to visit the Granger Stage Station is in the spring, summer, or fall.

Pass/Permit/Fees: There is no fee to visit the station.

Closest City or Town: Little America

Physical Address:
110 Spruce Street
Granger, WY 82934

GPS Coordinates: 41.59063° N, 109.97009° W

Did You Know? Two famous Americans who passed through the Granger Stage Station were Mark Twain and Horace Greeley, editor of the *New York Tribune.*

Little America

This tiny town (population 68) took its name from the Little America Motel, which was purposely built in a remote location as a haven to travelers who would have trouble finding lodging anywhere else close by. Built in 1934 by Stephen Mack Covey, the Little America Motel is named after Admiral Richard Byrd's base camp in Antarctica, which was also considered a haven in a harsh climate. The original motel had 12 cabins, two gas pumps, and a 24-seat café. Eventually, the Palm Room, a small bar and cocktail lounge, was added to the facilities.

Best Time to Visit: Little America is excellent to visit any time of the year.

Pass/Permit/Fees: There is no fee to visit Little America unless you stay overnight. Hotel room rates vary.

Closest City or Town: Little America

Physical Address:
I-80 Exit 68
Little America, WY 82929

GPS Coordinates: 41.55470° N, 109.86104° W

Did You Know? Stephen Mack Covey was a sheepherder who got lost in a snowstorm and had to spend the night outside in -40°F weather. He vowed to create a haven for others caught in similar circumstances in the future. The result was the Little America Motel, which eventually launched a successful chain of motels throughout the west.

Lost Springs

This tiny town in Converse County, believed to be the smallest incorporated town in the U.S., has a population of four. When it was first established as a town in 1911, it had about 200 residents, most of whom worked at the local Rosin coal mine. Eventually, in 1930, the coal mine closed, and most Lost Springs residents moved elsewhere for more job opportunities. While it may seem like there isn't much to do in a town this size, there are actually several activities worth your while. There is the Douglas Golf Course, the Pioneer Memorial Museum, the Stagecoach Museum, the Douglas Railroad Interpretive Museum at Locomotive Park, the House of Pinz bowling alley, and several bars and pubs.

Best Time to Visit: The best time to visit Lost Springs is in the spring, summer, or fall.

Pass/Permit/Fees: There is no fee to visit Lost Springs.

Closest City or Town: Lost Springs

Physical Address:
Converse County Tourism Board
121 Brownfield Road
Douglas, WY 82633

GPS Coordinates: 42.76510° N, 104.92626° W

Did You Know? Lost Springs got its name in the 1880s when railroad workers who were not able to find the springs that were marked on survey maps of the area decided to settle in the location that would eventually become the town.

Bighorn Canyon

Bighorn Canyon offers numerous opportunities for recreation in the natural world. Across more than 120,000 acres, visitors can experience diverse ecosystems, view abundant wildlife, and learn about more than 10,000 years of human history. More than 12 hiking trails are available in Bighorn Canyon, ranging from easy to challenging to accommodate hikers of all abilities. There are also plenty of fishing and boating opportunities, especially on Bighorn Lake, which is spectacularly surrounded by the 1,000-foot cliffs of Bighorn Canyon. Other activities that are popular in Bighorn Canyon include horseback riding, camping, snowshoeing, cross-country skiing, sledding, and ice fishing.

Best Time to Visit: Bighorn Canyon is excellent to visit year round.

Pass/Permit/Fees: There is no fee to visit the canyon.

Closest City or Town: Lovell

Physical Address:
Bighorn Canyon National Recreation Area
20 US-14
Lovell, WY 82431

GPS Coordinates: 45.06530° N, 108.24508° W

Did You Know? The Bighorn Canyon was carved over 5 million years by the Wind River, which turns into the Bighorn River at the Wedding of the Waters near the Wyoming town of Thermopolis.

Fossil Bone Cabin

Built in 1932 and intended to be a roadside attraction, the Fossil Bone Cabin is constructed entirely out of dinosaur bones. The cabin was the idea of Thomas Boylan, who originally homesteaded in this area in 1908. He initially wanted to build and display a full dinosaur skeleton to get travelers to stop at his gas station, but he didn't have enough bones from nearby Como Bluff to make this happen. Instead, he decided to build a house with his fossils, creating a structure out of 5,796 bones. He then printed postcards that travelers could purchase that advertised the cabin as "the strangest building in the world"; "the building that used to walk"; and "the world's oldest building." Currently, the cabin is closed to the public, but it can still be visited and used as a unique backdrop for photographs.

Best Time to Visit: The best time to visit the Fossil Bone Cabin is during the day in the spring, summer, or fall.

Pass/Permit/Fees: There is no fee to visit the cabin.

Closest City or Town: Medicine Bow

Physical Address:
Medicine Bow Museum and Visitor Center
405 Lincoln Highway
Medicine Bow, WY 82329

GPS Coordinates: 41.86538° N, 106.07299° W

Did You Know? The Fossil Bone Cabin weighs an estimated 102,116 pounds.

Grand Teton National Park

This 310,000-acre national park in northwestern Wyoming is located in the 40-mile-long Teton Mountain Range and includes the famous valley known as Jackson Hole. Before it was established as a national park in 1929, Grand Teton National Park was a popular fur-trading region in the early 1800s. Even today, Grand Teton National Park has an almost perfect ecosystem that has fostered the same species of flora and fauna since prehistoric times. There are over 1,000 species of plants, 300 species of birds, at least a dozen species of fish, and plenty of species of mammals that call the park home. Popular activities in Grand Teton National Park including mountaineering, fishing, camping, and hiking. It is a globally recognized area for trout fishing.

Best Time to Visit: The best time to visit Grand Teton National Park is in the spring or summer.

Pass/Permit/Fees: There is a $35 fee for a 7-day pass to enter Grand Teton National Park.

Closest City or Town: Moose

Physical Address:
Craig Thomas Discovery and Visitor Center
1 Teton Park Road
Moose, WY 83012

GPS Coordinates: 43.79244° N, 110.68589° W

Did You Know? Rocks found in Grand Teton National Park are the oldest found in any national park at 2.7 billion years of age.

Green River Lakes

Green River Lakes is one of Wyoming's most scenic drives. The lakes along this drive are located about 50 miles north of Pinedale and serve as the source of the Green River. As these lakes are filled with glacial water, they are too cold for swimming and most other water sports. Instead, the endpoint of the scenic journey to Green River Lakes provides travelers with a spectacular, often-photographed panorama of Squaretop Mountain towering over the Green River Lakes. Depending on the time of day you visit, you're likely to see elk, deer, moose, bears, eagles, and hawks, along with small wildlife. In the fall, the aspen trees provide an incredible show of color, especially when contrasted with the evergreen pine.

Best Time to Visit: The best time to visit Green River Lakes is in the fall when the leaves of the aspen trees are changing colors.

Pass/Permit/Fees: There is no fee to visit.

Closest City or Town: Pinedale

Physical Address:
Visit Pinedale
69 Pinedale South Road
Pinedale, WY 82941

GPS Coordinates: 43.27404° N, 109.82243° W

Did You Know? In October, the Green River Lakes is host to the Green River Drift, one of the lengthiest cattle drives in distance and the longest-running cattle drive in the country.

Heart Mountain Interpretive Center

The Heart Mountain Interpretive Center opened in 2011 as a way to preserve the remnants of the site of the Word War II internment camp for Japanese Americans in Park County. It serves to tell the stories of those who were incarcerated at the camp through artifacts, photographs, interactive exhibits, and oral histories. Visitors experience what it was like to live at Heart Mountain as a Japanese citizen or Japanese American who was forced to move to the camp in response to the Japanese attack on Pearl Harbor. Emphasis is placed on the diverse experiences of Japanese Americans in the camp, the Constitutional issues, the violations of civil rights and liberties, and the broader subjects of social justice and race in the U.S.

Best Time to Visit: The center is open daily between May 16 and October 2 from 10:00 a.m. to 5:00 p.m. The rest of the year, the center is only open Wednesday through Saturday during the same hours.

Pass/Permit/Fees: Admission is $12 for adults and $10 for seniors or students. Children under the age of 12 are free.

Closest City or Town: Powell

Physical Address:
1539 Road 19
Powell, WY 82435

GPS Coordinates: 44.67058° N, 108.94137° W

Did You Know? There were over 14,000 people incarcerated at the internment camp that is now the Heart Mountain Interpretive Center.

Wyoming Buckshot Saloon

At the base of the Bighorn Mountains, the Wyoming Buckshot Saloon is a place where travelers, wanderers, and locals alike can relax. Prior to 2016, the saloon was housed in the gas station next door, but its popularity mandated that it move to a larger location. Its once-small menu of local favorites like the Buff Chick came over too and are still a staple on today's expanded menu. The Wyoming Buckshot Saloon has long been a significant presence in the Ranchester community, and it continues to serve its hardworking residents with classic American cuisine that includes everything from Beer Tots to Cowboy Nachos, Roper's Chili to the Spicy! Buckfire burger.

Best Time to Visit: The grill at the Wyoming Buckshot Saloon is open daily from 10:00 a.m. to 10:00 p.m. The bar is open Sunday through Thursday from 10:00 a.m. to 11:00 p.m. and Friday and Saturday from 10:00 a.m. to 2:00 a.m.

Pass/Permit/Fees: There is no fee to visit the saloon, but be sure to bring money if you intend to eat or drink.

Closest City or Town: Ranchester

Physical Address:
719 Dayton Street
Ranchester, WY 82839

GPS Coordinates: 44.90884° N, 107.16952° W

Did You Know? A common phrase heard at the Wyoming Buckshot Saloon is "Want it dirty?" This is referring to its fries or tots and whether you want them smothered in homemade beer cheese and brown gravy.

Wyoming Frontier Prison Museum

Construction began on Wyoming's first state penitentiary, the Wyoming Frontier Prison, in 1888, but weather and funding issues delayed its opening until 1901. There were 104 cells, no running water, no electricity, and very little heating. In 1904, overcrowding became an issue, and 32 additional cells were added to the initial cell block. A second full cell block that included solitary confinement cells was added in 1950, and along with it came improved heating and running hot water. A dungeon, a "punishing pole," and various execution methods made this frontier prison a feared institution. A "death house," or death row, was added in 1916, which not only included six death-row cells but also indoor gallows. When the gas chamber replaced hanging as the state execution method, one was added to the death house.

Best Time to Visit: The Wyoming Frontier Prison Museum is open Monday through Thursday from 9:00 a.m. to 12:00 p.m. and 1:00 p.m. to 4:00 p.m.

Pass/Permit/Fees: There is no fee to visit the museum.

Closest City or Town: Rawlins

Physical Address:
500 West Walnut
Rawlins, WY 82301

GPS Coordinates: 41.79386° N, 107.24302° W

Did You Know? Prisoners at the Wyoming Frontier Prison produced brooms, shirts, woolen goods, and license plates at various times throughout its 80-year history.

Castle Gardens

Castle Gardens gets its name from its eroded and weather-beaten towering rocks that resemble castle turrets. The unique rock shapes have attracted visitors for thousands of years, and Native Americans carved evidence of their presence into the rocks, leaving well-preserved petroglyphs. The most famous of petroglyphs at Castle Gardens are the shield-style impressions that are the oldest depictions of warriors bearing shields. These petroglyphs also combine various manufacturing techniques that distinguish this art as unique in the Wind River and Bighorn basins. There are also depictions of shields alone, which is rare in Native American art. Castle Gardens first opened to the public in the 1960s in an attempt to stem the vandalism that was occurring in the area, including the theft of major works of rock art.

Best Time to Visit: The best time to visit Castle Gardens is during the spring, summer, or fall.

Pass/Permit/Fees: There is no fee to visit Castle Gardens.

Closest City or Town: Riverton

Physical Address:
1335 Main Street
Lander, WY 82520

GPS Coordinates: 42.93616° N, 107.61818° W

Did You Know? The petroglyph named the Great Turtle was chiseled out of the rock at Castle Gardens and stolen in 1940. It was anonymously returned to the State Museum a year later, and it remains there to this day.

Boar's Tusk

Boar's Tusk is an isolated geological formation that juts 400 feet above the surrounding plain to reach a peak elevation of 7,101 feet. It is the remnant of a long-extinct volcano that resembles the tusk of a wild boar. It is approximately 2.5 million years old and has been used as a landmark for travelers since before Europeans arrived. In addition to being the tallest structure for miles around, Boar's Tusk is also a mystery because of its green color. No one seems to know why it's green, and scientists don't seem to be in a hurry to figure it out due to its remoteness and the ruggedness of the area. The formation was once the magma chamber of an extremely large volcano. The area surrounding Boar's Tusk is popular with visitors in search of precious stones, but the existence of precious stones is really just a rumor. They won't find any diamonds here, but they may be able to unearth some semiprecious stones like amethyst and peridot.

Best Time to Visit: Boar's Tusk is open year round.

Pass/Permit/Fees: There is no fee to visit Boar's Tusk.

Closest City or Town: Rock Springs

Physical Address:
Explore Rock Springs & Green River Visitor Center
1641 Elk Street
Rock Springs, WY 82901

GPS Coordinates: 41.96592° N, 109.19803° W

Did You Know? Boar's Tusk is a popular place for rock climbers to challenge their skills.

Red Desert

Located in south-central Wyoming, the Red Desert is 9,320 square miles of high-altitude desert and sagebrush landscape that is home to the Killpecker Sand Dunes, the largest living dune system in the U.S. Despite its dryness and lack of vegetation, the desert is home to the largest migratory herd of pronghorn in the lower 48 states as well as various other wildlife. While the land is the largest unfenced area in the U.S., it is interrupted by various oil and gas roads, as the area holds an abundance of underground resources such as uranium, coal, natural gas, and oil. There is evidence of human habitation in the Red Desert dating back 12,000 years, including rock art found at Boars Tusk, Seedskadee, and East Flaming Gorge.

Best Time to Visit: The best time to visit the Red Desert is in the spring, summer, or fall.

Pass/Permit/Fees: There is no fee to visit the Red Desert.

Closest City or Town: Rock Springs

Physical Address:
Explore Rock Springs & Green River Visitor Center
1641 Elk Street
Rock Springs, WY 82901

GPS Coordinates: 41.61221° N, 109.23099

Did You Know? More than 2,000 natural gas wells dot the Red Desert, the result of the most recent energy-industry boom in Wyoming.

The Flaming Gorge

Named for its stunning red canyon walls, the Flaming Gorge is a national recreation area that encompasses 207,363 acres of scenic wilderness. The most popular Flaming Gorge attraction is Flaming Gorge Reservoir, which spans the states of Wyoming and Utah. The Green River is another favorite place to visit, as is the Flaming Gorge Dam and power plant, which is open for public tours. Common activities in the Flaming Gorge include fishing, water skiing, river tubing, boating, kayaking, hiking, mountain biking, and camping. Anglers can expect to catch a wide range of fish in the reservoir, including Burbot, common carp, rainbow trout, brown trout, smallmouth bass, and Kokanee salmon.

Best Time to Visit: The best time to visit the Flaming Gorge is in the summer, but it will be crowded. Try the spring or fall for fewer crowds.

Pass/Permit/Fees: There is no fee to visit the gorge, but a Recreation Use Pass is required to use the boat launches.

Closest City or Town: Rock Springs

Physical Address:
Explore Rock Springs & Green River Visitor Center
1641 Elk Street
Rock Springs, WY 82901

GPS Coordinates: 41.11619° N, 109.54066° W

Did You Know? The Flaming Gorge was named by explorer John Wesley Powell in 1869.

Saratoga Hot Springs Resort

Located between the Snowy Mountain Range and the Sierra Madre Mountain Range on the Upper North Platte River, the Saratoga Hot Springs Resort is a world-class mineral hot springs and spa destination. The history of the location begins more than 145 years ago as a log building that housed a post office, general store, saloon, community center, gambling hall, bathhouse, and bar. It later became the Saratoga Hot Springs Hotel, then the State Hot Springs Reserve, and then the Saratoga Inn. Finally, it was named the Saratoga Hot Springs Resort when it was purchased by famous surgeon Michael Janssen in 2008. It has undergone extensive remodeling throughout the years, but many original components of the resort remain, including the barn wood in the main lodge and the gneiss rock wall in the banquet rooms and lobby.

Best Time to Visit: The resort is open year round.

Pass/Permit/Fees: The fees for the resort depend on room and date selection. See the resort's website for pricing details.

Closest City or Town: Saratoga

Physical Address:
601 Pic Pike Road
Saratoga, WY 82331

GPS Coordinates: 41.45313° N, 106.80129° W

Did You Know? The original Saratoga Hot Springs Hotel had a barber shop, drug store, 60-person dining room, a ladies reception room, a hotel office, and a billiard room.

Fetterman Battlefield

A monument to the second-worst U.S. Army defeat by Plains Indians sits on the site of what was once the Fetterman Battlefield. The monument, which was erected in the 1930s, and a walking trail with more than 30 interpretive signs tell the story of Captain William J. Fetterman, who, in 1886, was lured to the area by Crazy Horse to save a wagon train from Indian attacks. Fetterman was not supposed to go over Lodge Trail Ridge, which put him out of sight of the fort, but Fetterman was not one to take orders and believed he had an army that could take on the "whole Sioux Nation." Just as he and his men passed the ridge, over 1,000 Cheyenne, Lakota Sioux, and Arapaho warriors attacked the men. In just a half an hour, all 81 members of Fetterman's group were killed.

Best Time to Visit: The best time to visit Fetterman Battlefield is during the spring, summer, or fall.

Pass/Permit/Fees: There is no fee to visit the battlefield.

Closest City or Town: Sheridan

Physical Address:
Sheridan Travel & Tourism
1517 E. 5th Street
Sheridan, WY 82801

GPS Coordinates: 44.63177° N, 106.84949° W

Did You Know? The Fetterman Battle took place on Crow land that the U.S. government had promised them. The Lakota, Cheyenne, and Arapaho were enemies of the Crow and ignored the treaty that gave them the land.

Shell Falls

This waterfall is one of the main attractions in Bighorn National Forest and it is often referred to as the "thundering heartbeat of the Bighorn Mountains." While only 75 feet tall, Shell Falls is a fast-flowing waterfall that drops at a rate of 3,600 gallons per second. It was formed by a fault line that caused one side of the fault to thrust upward and the other side to drop downward. The water now follows the fracture as it cascades over the ledge. This formation is different from how waterfalls are normally created, which makes it a unique sight to see.

There is also an Interpretive Center and Museum near the falls that provides information and exhibits explaining the interesting geology in the area. The center offers a short, groomed trail that culminates in a viewing platform.

Best Time to Visit: The best time to visit Shell Falls is in the spring, summer, or fall.

Pass/Permit/Fees: There is no fee to visit Shell Falls.

Closest City or Town: Sheridan

Physical Address:
Sheridan Travel & Tourism
1517 E. 5th Street
Sheridan, WY 82801

GPS Coordinates: 44.58806° N, 107.61376° W

Did You Know? Shell Falls gets its name from the fossils of seashells imbedded in the canyon walls, which suggests the area was once under an ancient ocean.

Trail End

This historic house museum built in the Flemish Revival style faithfully represents life as it was in Wyoming between 1913 and 1933. Trail End was the home of John B. Kendrick, a former Wyoming governor and U.S. senator. He had the house built between 1908 and 1913 when he, his wife Eula Wulfjen Kendrick, and their two children Rosa-Maye and Manville moved in. They didn't live there very long before Kendrick was elected governor and moved to Cheyenne, then to Washington, D.C. when he was elected senator. The family used Trail End primarily as a summer home until Kendrick died in 1933. Eula made Trail End her primary home from 1933 to 1961. Eventually, the house was abandoned until 1968 when it was converted into a community museum.

Best Time to Visit: Trail End is open daily between June 1 and August 31 from 9:00 a.m. to 6:00 p.m. Hours vary during the rest of the year. Check the website for details.

Pass/Permit/Fees: The fee to visit Trail End is $4 for adults ages 18 and older or $2 for Wyoming residents. Children ages 17 and under are free.

Closest City or Town: Sheridan

Physical Address:
400 Clarendon Avenue
Sheridan, WY 82801

GPS Coordinates: 45.02709° N, 106.96530° W

Did You Know? Trail End was designed by architect Glenn Charles MacAlister and cost $164,000.

South Pass

South Pass is actually two mountain passes located on the
Continental Divide. It lies between the Wind River Range
and the Oregon Buttes. It's the lowest point on the
Continental Divide between the Southern and Central
Rocky Mountains, but it's still a mile and a half above sea
level. The natural route over the mountains became the path
for travelers on the California, Oregon, and Mormon trails
in the 19th century. The pass was already well-known to
Native Americans by the time it was first crossed by Robert
Stuart and six companions in 1812. The group was trying to
stay out of the way of Crow warriors further north as they
returned from a fur-trading trip. Stuart learned of the pass
from a Shoshone tribe member, something that was
withheld from the Lewis and Clark expedition that took
place from 1803 to 1806. Stuart's "discovery" went
unexplored for over a decade due to the War of 1812.

Best Time to Visit: The best time to visit South Pass is in
the spring, summer, or fall.

Pass/Permit/Fees: There is no fee to visit South Pass.

Closest City or Town: South Pass City

Physical Address:
South Pass City Historic Site
125 S. Pass Main Street
South Pass City, WY 82520

GPS Coordinates: 42.37325° N, 10891448° W

Did You Know? By 1860, 300,000 Americans had crossed
South Pass on their way to the West.

116

Aladdin Coal Tipple

The Aladdin Coal Tipple is a wooden structure that was used at one of Wyoming's coal mines to store and sort coal as it moved down the chutes. It is one of the few wooden tipples left in the American West. Constructed and used in the 1800s, the Aladdin Coal Tipple was part of many mining operations in the valley, but when the nearby railroad closed, Aladdin became one of the last companies to survive, lasting until 1942. While visitors aren't able to get too close to the structure today because of its instability, there is a walking path around the perimeter fence and informational signage that provides interesting facts about both Wyoming's mining past and the Aladdin Coal Tipple specifically. This tipple is a prime example of mine-engineering technology from the late 1800s and early 1900s.

Best Time to Visit: The Aladdin Coal Tipple is open for visitors year round.

Pass/Permit/Fees: There is no fee to visit.

Closest City or Town: Sundance

Physical Address:
Northeast Wyoming Welcome Center
5266 Old Highway 14
Beulah, WY 82712

GPS Coordinates: 44.63896° N, 104.16335° W

Did You Know? The coal mined at the Aladdin Coal Tipple was used to fire the gold smelters in Deadwood, South Dakota and as a local fuel source.

The Quaal Windsock

Driving across the plains of Wyoming can be a little boring, but luckily Mick and Jean Quaal did something about that and turned an early 1950s Beechcraft Twin Bonanza airplane into a windsock that can be seen from miles around. A windsock, which normally looks like a cloth cone flying from a pole, is used to show the direction in which the wind is blowing. They are often seen in windy places like Wyoming, where the vast open spaces create the perfect environment for some of the most powerful wind gusts in the nation.

The Quaals used a flatbed truck, a crane, and a group of people with ropes to hoist the plane to the top of a 70-foot pole. The bright yellow airplane spins around on the tall pole to indicate the direction the wind is blowing.

Best Time to Visit: The best time to visit the Quaal Windsock is during the day in the spring, summer, or fall.

Pass/Permit/Fees: There is no fee to visit.

Closest City or Town: Sundance

Physical Address:
Sundance Travel Center
2723 E. Cleveland Street
Sundance, WY 82729

GPS Coordinates: 44.51899° N. 104.21580° W

Did You Know? First flown in 1949 and produced in 1951, the Twin Bonanza used for the Quaal Windsock was once a utility transport plane for the U.S. Army.

Vore Buffalo Jump

The Vore Buffalo Jump has a morbid past, as it was once used by Native American hunters to drive stampeding bison over the edge of this steep-sided pit, which would kill or severely disable the bison, making them easier to skin and clean. According to buffalo bones found about 15 feet deep in the pit, the Vore Buffalo Jump pit was used as a kill site by the Kiowa and Apache Native American tribes from approximately 1500 to 1800 CE. The pit was discovered in the early 1970s when I-90 was under construction. The sinkhole was explored, large quantities of bison bones were found, and the University of Wyoming was called in to investigate further.

Best Time to Visit: This attraction is open daily between June 1 and August 22 from 8:00 a.m. to 6:00 p.m.

Pass/Permit/Fees: The fee to visit the Vore Buffalo Jump is $9 for adults ages 13 and older and $5 for children between the ages of 7 and 12. Children ages 6 and under are free.

Closest City or Town: Sundance

Physical Address:
369 Old U.S. 14
Sundance, WY 82729

GPS Coordinates: 44.53610° N, 104.15734° W

Did You Know? Only 5 percent of the Vore Buffalo Jump Pit has been excavated, and it is estimated to hold the remains of 20,000 buffalo.

Ten Sleep

At the base of the Bighorn Mountains sits the small town of Ten Sleep. Its primary industries are cattle and sheep ranching, but tourism comes in a close third. Ten Sleep is an excellent town to stay in while you take part in the numerous outdoor activities the surrounding community has to offer, including mountain climbing, rock climbing, hiking, camping, boating, fishing, hunting, horseback riding, skiing, and more. At one time, the Girl Scout National Center West was located in Ten Sleep, and at 15,00 acres, was one of the largest encampments in the world. The former Girl Scout site is now owned by the Nature Conservancy and operates as the Ten Sleep Preserve. The town's general store, Ten Sleep Mercantile, is reminiscent of a traditional small-town store and has been a focal point of the town since opening in 1905.

Best Time to Visit: The best time to visit Ten Sleep is during the summer, especially around the 4th of July.

Pass/Permit/Fees: There is no fee to visit Ten Sleep.

Closest City or Town: Ten Sleep

Physical Address:
Town of Ten Sleep
415 5th Street
Ten Sleep, WY 82442

GPS Coordinates: 44.03716° N, 107.44645° W

Did You Know? The name of Ten Sleep comes from being 10 nights away, or midway, between two Sioux Camps, one on the Platte River and one near Bridger, Montana.

Big Horn Hot Springs State Reserve

Due to the reported therapeutic nature of hot springs, the Big Horn Hot Springs State Reserve was designated Wyoming's first state park in 1897. It quickly attracted tourists who were in search of the healing waters. The Northern Arapahoe and Eastern Shoshone Native American tribes sold the land to the U.S. government and in the process secured an agreement that access to the mineral hot springs would always be free to the public.

As such, a free bathhouse is still available and open year round. While you're visiting the state reserve, you'll likely catch a glimpse of the Hot Springs State Park bison herd that has lived at the park since 1916. To ensure they have enough to eat during the late fall and winter months, the buffalo are fed a daily supplement.

Best Time to Visit: The public bathhouse at the reserve is open Monday through Saturday from 8:00 a.m. to 5:30 p.m. and on Sunday from 12:00 p.m. to 5:30 p.m.

Pass/Permit/Fees: There is no fee to visit.

Closest City or Town: Thermopolis

Physical Address:
220 Park Street
Thermopolis, WY 82443

GPS Coordinates: 43.65070° N, 108.20495° W

Did You Know? The Big Horn River flows from the springs at Big Horn Hot Springs State Reserve at a rate of 18,000 gallons per day.

Star Plunge Water Park

Located in Hot Springs State Park in Thermopolis, Star Plunge Water Park is good for the body and soul. Visitors can warm up in the winter or cool off in the summer, all the while benefiting from the natural minerals in the hot springs. Activities available at the park include water slides, an indoor pool, an outdoor pool, hot tubs, water jets, a steam cave, a fountain waterfall, and a baby pool, among other attractions. There is also a snack bar and a gift shop on site. A water park of sorts has been located here since 1900, when the first Star Plunge was a simple canvas-topped hole in the springs. The structure would sometimes be drained to hold church services, speeches, and boxing matches.

Best Time to Visit: Star Plunge Water Park is open daily year round from 9:00 a.m. to 9:00 p.m.

Pass/Permit/Fees: The fee to visit Star Plunge Water Park is $15.50 for guests ages 5 to 64, $7 for children ages 4 and under, and $12.50 for seniors ages 65 and older.

Closest City or Town: Thermopolis

Physical Address:
115 Big Springs Drive
Thermopolis, WY 82443

GPS Coordinates: 43.65213° N, 108.19553° W

Did You Know? Towels and bathing suits can be rented at Star Plunge Water Park for $3 per item plus a $1 refundable deposit. Balls are $1 and tubes are $2.

Wind River Canyon

Situated between the Wyoming towns of Thermopolis and Shoshoni, Wind River Canyon is accessible by Wyoming Highway 789 and U.S. Highway 20, a route that was designated as a scenic byway in 2005. Gorgeous views of Chimney Rock, the Owl Creek Mountains, Boysen Reservoir, and the pink cliffs themselves make this canyon drive one of the most spectacular in the state.

The canyon is also a popular place for hiking, backpacking, camping, fishing, whitewater rafting, canoeing, kayaking, rock climbing, and horseback riding. Jet skiing and water skiing on the 19,000-acre Boysen Reservoir are other favorite water activities. Some of the best trout fishing in the country can be found in the Wind River Canyon in Wind River, which becomes the Rocky Mountain Bighorn River at the Wedding of the Waters.

Best Time to Visit: The best time to visit Wind River Canyon is in the summer, especially for water activities.

Pass/Permit/Fees: There is no fee to visit the canyon.

Closest City or Town: Thermopolis

Physical Address:
Thermopolis-Hot Springs Visitor Center
220 Park Street
Thermopolis, WY 82443

GPS Coordinates: 43.58163° N, 108.21322° W

Did You Know? Driving the Wind River Canyon is rated the top thing to do in Thermopolis by TripAdvisor.

Wyoming Dinosaur Center

Home to one of the world's largest and most diverse fossil collections, the Wyoming Dinosaur Center is one of the few dinosaur museums that has excavation sites within driving distance. The main dig sites are located on the Warm Springs Ranch and have yielded more than 10,000 dinosaur bones, many of which are now on display at the museum. More than 50 mounted dinosaur skeletons are available for viewing, including a full *Supersaurus vivianae* that was excavated from a nearby Douglas quarry.

Best Time to Visit: The center is open between May 15 and September 14 from 8:00 a.m. to 6:00 p.m. and between September 15 and May 14 from 10:00 a.m. to 5:00 p.m.

Pass/Permit/Fees: The fee to visit the Wyoming Dinosaur Center is $12 for adults or $2 for Thermopolis residents. Seniors ages 65 and older, veterans, and children between the ages of 4 and 12 are eligible for a discounted rate of $10.

Closest City or Town: Thermopolis

Physical Address:
110 Carter Ranch Road
Thermopolis, WY 82443

GPS Coordinates: 43.64346° N, 108.20046° W

Did You Know? The *Supersaurus vivianae* skeleton on display at the Wyoming Dinosaur Center is named Jimbo and is one of the most complete specimens ever found. It is 106 feet long and was donated to the museum in 2003.

Proper Planning

With this guide, you are well on your way to properly planning a marvelous adventure. When you plan your travels, you should become familiar with the area, save any maps to your phone for access without internet, and bring plenty of water—especially during the summer months. Depending on which adventure you choose, you will also want to bring snacks or even a lunch. For younger children, you should do your research and find destinations that best suit your family's needs. You should also plan when and where to get gas, local lodgings, and food. We've done our best to group these destinations based on nearby towns and cities to help make planning easier.

Dangerous Wildlife

There are several dangerous animals and insects you may encounter while hiking. With a good dose of caution and awareness, you can explore safely. Here are steps you can take to keep yourself and your loved ones safe from dangerous flora and fauna while exploring:

- Keep to the established trails.
- Do not look under rocks, leaves, or sticks.
- Keep hands and feet out of small crawl spaces, bushes, covered areas, or crevices.
- Wear long sleeves and pants to keep arms and legs protected.
- Keep your distance should you encounter any dangerous wildlife or plants.

Limited Cell Service

Do not rely on cell service for navigation or emergencies. Always have a map with you and let someone know where you are and how long you intend to be gone, just in case.

First Aid Information

Always travel with a first aid kit in case of emergencies.

Here are items you should be certain to include in your primary first aid kit:

- Nitrile gloves
- Blister care products
- Band-Aids in multiple sizes and waterproof type
- Ace wrap and athletic tape
- Alcohol wipes and antibiotic ointment
- Irrigation syringe
- Tweezers, nail clippers, trauma shears, safety pins
- Small zip-lock bags containing contaminated trash

It is recommended to also keep a secondary first aid kit, especially when hiking, for more serious injuries or medical emergencies. Items in this should include:

- Blood clotting sponges
- Sterile gauze pads
- Trauma pads

- Second-skin/burn treatment
- Triangular bandages/sling
- Butterfly strips
- Tincture of benzoin
- Medications (ibuprofen, acetaminophen, antihistamine, aspirin, etc.)
- Thermometer
- CPR mask
- Wilderness medicine handbook
- Antivenin

There is much more to explore, but this is a great start.

For information on all national parks, visit https://www.nps.gov/index.htm .

This site will give you information on up-to-date entrance fees and how to purchase a park pass for unlimited access to national and state parks. This site will also introduce you to all of the trails at each park.

Always check before you travel to destinations to make sure there are no closures. Some hiking trails close when there is heavy rain or snow in the area and other parks close parts of their land for the migration of wildlife. Attractions may change their hours or temporarily shut down for various reasons. Check the websites for the most up-to-date information.